Language Development for Science

Other titles in the series:

Language Development
Circle Time Sessions to Improve Communication Skills
Marion Nash with Jackie Lowe and Tracey Palmer
1-84312-156-5

Language Development
Activities for Home
Marion Nash and Jackie Lowe
1-84312-170-0

Language Development for Maths
Circle Time Sessions to Improve Language Skills
Marion Nash and Jackie Lowe
1-84312-171-9

Language Development for Maths
Activities for Home
Marion Nash and Jackie Lowe
1-84312-172-7

Language Development for Science
Activities for Home
Marion Nash and Jackie Lowe
1-84312-174-3

Language Development for Science

Circle Time Sessions to Improve Language Skills in Science

Marion Nash and Jackie Lowe

 David Fulton Publishers

David Fulton Publishers Ltd
The Chiswick Centre, 414 Chiswick High Road, London W4 5TF

www.fultonpublishers.co.uk

First published in Great Britain in 2005 by David Fulton Publishers

10 9 8 7 6 5 4 3 2 1

Note: The right of the individual contributors to be identified as the authors of their work has been asserted by them in accordance with the Copyright, Designs and Patents Act, 1988.

Copyright © Marion Nash and Jackie Lowe 2005

Illustrations by Phillipa Drakeford.

British Library Cataloguing in Publication Data
A catalogue record for this book is available from the British Library.

ISBN: 1-84312-173-5

David Fulton Publishers is a division of Granada Learning Limited, part of ITV plc.

The materials in this publication may be photocopied only for use within the purchasing organisation. Otherwise, all rights reserved. No part of this publication may be reproduced, stored in a retrieval system or transmitted, in any form or by any means, electronic, mechanical, photocopying, or otherwise, without the prior permission of the publishers.

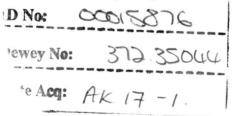

Typeset by FiSH Books, London
Printed and bound in Great Britain

Contents

To my partner David with many thanks, Tom and Angie
and to the weezles.

Acknowledgments

The publication of this book has been made possible by the foresight and support of the people who work in the Plymouth Education Authority and those who direct it. The work has been supported and encouraged by Bronwen Lacy, Director for Lifelong Learning and Maggie Carter, Head of Service (Learner Support) and Kevin Rowland, Principal Educational Psychologist, in line with their commitment to enrich the educational experiences of children in the City of Plymouth. As a result, many children in other areas will have the opportunity to grow in confidence and develop new skills through working with the materials.

Ford Primary School in Plymouth is at the heart of the development of this book. Many thanks to the Head, staff (in particular Val Galer who continues the important work of running the groups); also governors and parents. Thanks particularly to the children who were the initial inspiration for the work. Highfield Primary School in Plymouth has played an increasingly important role in supporting the development of Spirals. Many thanks to Paddy Marsh, the Head; Linda Mercer, the SENCO; and the staff, parents and children. I have also recently found a great deal of interest and inspiration from the ideas of Jenny Mosley, Ann Locke, and David Leah (Student Support Manager, Plymouth College of Further Education).

Special thanks to Linda Evans (Fulton) for her interest, enthusiasm and guidance. Many thanks to Jenny and Geoff who made the accompanying video material. Their professionalism, patience and good humour made working with them great fun. A thank you to ICAN who have supported the training at a national level.

Thanks to the Plymouth Educational Psychology team, and in particular Mick Johnson for his much appreciated support and enthusiasm for the Spirals work. Special thanks to the admin team, especially Sally and Liz.

Many thanks to my partner David, whose creative formatting skills and warm support have been invaluable; also to my family and especially my grandson Tom who provided the original inspiration for this series of books.

This book contains many traditional and tried and true materials and if I have omitted to attribute material to anybody it is not intentional, and I hereby take this opportunity to thank them.

Marion Nash, Educational Psychologist

Video CD and training

There is a short video recorded on to a CD contained in this pack. This features Educational Psychologist Marion Nash and Speech and Language Therapist Jackie Lowe describing the Spirals programme. There are also extracts from a Spirals session run in Ford Primary School with SENCO Val Gaylor, and teacher Cecilia Harris of Ford Primary School demonstrating the small group Circle Time approach. It also demonstrates the use of some of the sung rhymes. This will be a useful resource for schools preparing to use the Spirals materials and is easily accessed by the CD drive in your computer. Marion Nash offers popular training courses nationally through the ICAN speech and language organisation (details available through www.Ican.org.uk/ professionaldevelopment; tel. 0845 225 4073).

Marion offers training in Spirals Language and Spirals Maths as well as Spirals Science. Marion also offers courses on effective use of puppets for learning.

Courses tailored to your needs can be developed. Please contact marion_m_nash@msn.com for more details or see www.spiralstraining.co.uk.

The video CD has been made by Jeff Booth of Highfield Productions (tel. 01548 830274).

Introduction

Spirals Science came about largely because of the success of our initial language development programme (*Language Development: Circle Time Sessions to Improve Communication Skills*; see pages 112–3 for details). The programme is based on the Circle Time ethos, which has been widely promoted by Leslie Button, Jenny Mosley and others in recent years. In 2000/2001, I worked alongside Jackie Lowe, a senior Speech and Language Therapist, and teacher Tracey Palmer, to plan a series of carefully crafted sessions to develop language skills and thinking skills in linguistically vulnerable children. Before long, schools trialling the sessions were reporting pleasing gains made by the children involved. Teachers were observing gains made on several fronts:

- listening and concentration skills;
- expressive and receptive language;
- confidence and self-esteem.

These gains were also seen to transfer to the large group/classroom situation and evidence is now emerging of a positive effect on progress in reading as well.

This success is undoubtedly due, at least in part, to the supportive Circle Time ethos as applied to the small group sessions. These are all planned to incorporate:

- movement for a purpose;
- talking and questioning;
- music, rhythm and rhyme;
- critical reasoning and thinking;
- social skills;
- emotional awareness.

After being asked to develop a similar scheme with maths vocabulary in mind, we produced a second set of materials which also proved to be very effective. We were then approached about developing a Science Spirals scheme. We took on the task enthusiastically and looked into establishing a course that would develop understanding and confident use of science-related vocabulary. We introduced a large element of verbal reasoning with an emphasis on investigating and exploring the world around the child. The demands that science makes for the understanding of exploratory language may be one of the underlying reasons why children struggle with it. One answer is to plan ways of presenting science concepts at the right level and in

1

different ways which will engage all learning styles, consolidate memory and recall, and help learners to bring all their strengths together on the task. Use of Spirals groups built around this system will enable a wide range of children to experience success in science in Key Stage 1 and beyond.

Parents and carers are key partners in the learning process for the child, and have responded enthusiastically to our Home Activities workbooks which accompany and support the Spirals language sessions, so naturally we have devised a third Home book to accompany the Spiral Science sessions. This outlines simple activities for supporting the work going on in school in a fun and stress-free way (details are on pages 112–3).

What happens in the group?

In a small group, we are able to be sensitive to the different learning and teaching styles of the children and the staff involved. Each session is crafted to provide a range of learning inputs.

- Each session is based on activities to promote reflection and critical thinking.
- The supportive principles of Circle Time are drawn upon to provide a group ethos in which we can foster the children's confidence in putting ideas forward. The sessions highlight the importance of 'brainstorming'; that is, allowing everyone to bring their ideas to a task before we select (but not judge) the most appropriate answer.
- The levels of activity and focus are carefully balanced to achieve motivation and optimum attention. The pace and language are deliberately slowed down. This has a tremendously positive impact on behaviour as children realise they can access the activities fully.
- The content of the sessions includes scientific concepts, but also thinking skills, prediction, reasoning, hypothesis developments and checking, and effective questioning.
- The sessions give opportunities for dynamic assessment of children's needs and progress which can be supplemented in class lessons.
- Listening and turn-taking are an integral part of the course.
- Visualisation and harnessing imagination are introduced as powerful learning tools.
- Speaking with confidence and clarity to an audience and communicating their thinking is an outcome that is carefully planned for.

The course as a whole prepares children for the transitions from learning from experience to learning from direct teaching by encouraging their ability to listen, to visualise an action, number or quantity, and to recall and describe events.

What are the effects of the group on children?

The children become much more skilled and effective thinkers and communicators. The group allows them to overcome the barriers to learning and to bring their 'heart, mind and hand' to the task. Learning is fun and relaxed, and therefore memorable and likely to endure and develop over time.

Children are highly motivated through the fun feeling to the group. They find they are concentrating almost without realising it, and contributing answers and ideas – perhaps for the first time since starting school.

In the small group we are able to keep the instructional language straightforward and not too demanding. The children blossom as they find that they can more easily understand the language, and slowly gain confidence in learning and talking in more formal situations.

Teachers often report that after only four sessions they see positive changes in children's attitudes and behaviour.

How to use this book

Who are the intended group?

- The course contained in this book has been developed to aid linguistically challenged children; children who find it difficult to understand verbal instructions and who do not have the skills or confidence to frame questions to clarify their understanding, or to speak out in a large group.
- The content relates to the language skills required to develop understanding of basic scientific concepts.
- The activities are designed to achieve a balance of movement and focus, to maintain concentration and to help achieve mastery – a range of concepts, skills and processes are developed through the games.
- Over and above this, the children develop confidence in themselves as learners – this confidence carries over to other situations including the classroom.

Before running the groups

1 Involve staff in discussion about the aims of the group and children who would benefit from inclusion in the group. Watch the accompanying video film together.
2 Involve parents and carers. Seek parental permission if an outside agency is involved in running the group with the school.
3 Assess: (a) take a snapshot of the children's strengths and difficulties with the individual assessment form provided on page 7, using one copy for each pupil; (b) plan targets for the group. Individual IEPs may be used where appropriate.
4 Identify two people who will be running the group. This is a necessity, not a luxury.

5 Create a box of resources to keep on hand for the group. Some materials are provided in the Appendices.

When running the groups

6 Record attendance at sessions (see page 6).
7 When the first session starts tell the children how special their group is. This is an opportunity to give lots of positive messages.
8 Follow the golden keys: Pause, Ponder, Use Praise Phrases, slow the Pace.
9 At the end of each half-term reassess the children on the scales you have chosen and review the group and individual targets.
10 For the final group session include a farewell followed up with drawings of things the children have especially enjoyed so that they have a concrete reminder for as long as they need it.

Using the materials: flexibility

When using the materials go by the level that you feel your group of children have reached. There will be some groups of children who need repetition of sessions and some groups who need to start sessions at a higher level.

All groups of children can vary in their needs and you may find that in one setting the children work happily at the earlier sessions whereas in another they have mastered the basic concepts therein and need to work on the concepts contained in the later sessions.

In our experience some sessions will need to be repeated three or more times, whereas another session at the same level is assimilated at the first presentation.

Further reading

Barnes, D. and Todd, G. (1977) *Language and Communication in Small Groups*. London: Routledge & Keegan Paul.

Cheshire County Council Website. www.salt.cheshire.gov.uk.

Gardener, H. (1993a) *Frames of Mind: The Theory of Multiple Intelligences*. Toronto: HarperCollins Canada.

Gardener, H. (1993b) *Multiple Intelligences: The Theory in Practice*. Toronto: HarperCollins Canada.

Goodlad, J. (1984) *A Place Called School: Prospects for the Future*. New York: McGraw-Hill.

Kann Yeok-Hwa, N. (1998) *Enhancing Student Thinking Through Collaborative Learning*. Eric Digests ED422586 (Internet).

Kemple, K.M. (1992) *Understanding and Facilitating Pre-school Children's Peer Acceptance*. Eric Digests ED345866 (Internet).

Mosley, J. (1993) *Turn Your School Round*. Cambridge: LDA.

Mosley, J. (1996) *Quality Circle Time in the Primary School*. Cambridge: LDA.

Sizer, T. (1984) *Horace's Compromise*. Boston, MA: Houghton Mifflin.

Resources

Science Rabbit which pops out of a felt cabbage and is available with various mini-beasts (and many more puppets) from:

The Puppet Company Ltd, Unit 2, CAM Centre, Wilbury Way, Hitchin, Hertfordshire SG4 0TW
Tel. 01462 446040
www.puppetsbypost.com

Spirals language development group attendance record

Date of session	Session no.	Run by	Children who attended

Name ....   **Class** ....

Please could you write a brief description about the child's present level of attainment in each of the following skills. You will be asked to repeat this activity in six weeks, therefore it would be helpful if, during the time, you could note any significant developments in any of the following areas and write them down.
Thank you.

Skill	Present level (1)	Present level (2)
Thinking skills Awareness and use of problem-solving strategies		
Language skills Ability to respond to questions		
Social skills Attitude and response towards peers		
Listening skills Ability to listen and concentrate in class/group situations		
Classroom Confidence, responses and general performance in the classroom		

Materials that need preparation prior to sessions

Session 1

- Picture of nose.
- Two small covered containers (e.g. one containing bath salts, the other orange peel).
- Smooth material such as a silk scarf.
- Feely bag containing smooth and rough/coarse materials.
- Safety hand mirror.

Session 2

- Two pots with different scents in each.
- Safety hand mirror.
- Tray of magnetic shapes.

Session 3

- Rabbit with movable paws and eyes or another animal puppet with all sense organs.
- Safety hand mirror.
- One rough and one smooth object.

Session 4

- Cardboard box containing a bell or other object which makes a noise.
- Rabbit with movable paws and eyes, or other animal puppet with all sense organs.
- Tray of magnetic shapes.

Session 5

- Magnetic shapes.
- Tin tray.
- Wooden board.
- Large book.

- Three post-it notes and felt-tip pen to record (optional).
- Rabbit puppet (eyes covered with a scarf).
- Safety hand mirror.

Session 6

- Shoe box with small hole in it.
- Torch.
- Small cloth for a blanket.
- Rabbit (animal) puppet.
- Pictures of night-time (see appendices).
- Two pieces of material (one dark, one light).
- Strong-smelling substance in a covered box into which a straw is inserted.

Session 7

- Three different fish shapes cut out from transparent material.
- Torch.
- Tray of magnetic shapes.
- Small cloth for a blanket.
- Pictures of night-time (see appendices).

Session 8

- Animal puppet.
- Feely bag.
- Jacket, sock, tie, scarf.
- Three different transparent fish shapes.
- One (opaque) fish shape.
- Torch.

Session 9

- Animal puppet.
- Pictures or real examples of hot and cold food.
- Safety hand mirror.
- Rabbit puppet with scarf over eyes.
- Four pieces of opaque material cut into the shape of a snake.
- Torch.

Session 10

- Magnetic shapes.
- Tin tray.
- Wooden board.
- Large book.
- Post-it notes and a pen to record (optional).
- Feely bag containing an unusually shaped solid object.
- Torch.
- Four pieces of material cut into the shape of a snake.

Session 11

- Pictures of night-time (see appendices).
- Picture of types of people who work at night.
- Instruments played by shaking them.
- Animal puppet.
- Pictures or real examples of hot and cold food.
- Pictures (or models) of a fridge and a cooker.
- Small cloth.

Session 12

- Tambourine and shaker bells.
- Three pull-along toys (these could include a large plastic or cardboard box).
- Pictures (or models) of a fridge and a cooker.
- Feely bag containing an unusually shaped solid object.
- Torch.

Session 13

- Tambourine.
- Wind instrument (e.g. whistle or flute).
- Selection of clear fish shapes.
- Selection of opaque snake shapes.
- Three push-along items (these could include a large plastic or cardboard box).
- Torch.

Session 14

- Something that will grow (e.g. cress seeds).
- Pictures of water, sun and items of food.
- Tambourine and bag made of thick material.
- Three items: a push-along toy, a pull-along toy with string attached and a large plastic or cardboard box.

Session 15

- Tambourine.
- Percussion instrument (e.g. drum).
- See-through fish and opaque snake.
- Cress seeds to check for growth.
- Torch.

Session 16

- Cress seeds to check for growth.
- Top up water.
- Dark box.
- Small cloth for a blanket.
- Pictures of night-time.
- Picture of types of people who work at night and their vehicles.
- Shaker bells and bag made of thick material.

Session 17

- Cress seeds to check for growth.
- Top up water.
- Tambourine and triangle or wooden beater.
- Animal puppet.
- Plastic cube.
- Science rabbit.
- See-through fish and opaque snake.
- Torch.

Session 18

- Cress seeds to check for growth.
- Top up water.
- Cube shape.
- Tambourine and shaker bells.
- Picture of nose (see appendix).
- Two small covered boxes containing two different scents (e.g. bath salts, orange peel).

Session 19

- Cress seeds to check for growth.
- Top up water.
- Tambourine and wooden beater or triangle (different from last time).
- Cube shape.
- Another shaken instrument.

Session 20

- Cress seeds to check for growth.
- Top up water.
- Magnetic shapes.
- Tin tray.
- Wooden board.
- Large box.
- Post-it notes and pen to record (optional).

- Science rabbit.
- 'Growing' picture cards.
- See-through fish and opaque snake shapes.
- Torch.

Session 21

- Tambourine or shaker bells.
- Three items: a push-along toy, a pull-along toy with string attached and a large plastic or cardboard box.
- Cress seeds to check for growth.
- Top up water.
- Cube shapes.
- Pictures of growing/non-growing things.

Session 22

- Pictures of toys (e.g. scooter, bicycle, skateboard).
- Feely bag containing pictures of fur- and feather-covered creatures, and people.
- Torch.

Session 23

- Tambourine.
- Triangle or wooden beater.
- Feely bag containing pictures of fur- and feather-covered creatures, and people.
- Two bar magnets.
- Safety hand mirror.

Session 24

- Tambourine or shaker bells.
- Two red and two white squares of any material for each group of children.
- Feely bag containing pictures of fur- and feather-covered creatures, and people.

Session 25

- Two bar magnets.
- Two jars containing water; salt and instant coffee.
- Stirrer.

Session 26

- Cardboard box (e.g. shoe box).
- Torch.
- Small cloth for a blanket.

- Pictures of night-time (see appendices).
- Two jars containing water; icing sugar, bicarbonate of soda.
- Stirrer.

Session 27

- A push-along toy, a pull-along toy with string attached, and six cube shapes.
- Two jars containing white vinegar, and salt and bicarbonate of soda.
- Stirrer.
- Coloured marbles in a jar.

Session 28

- Animal puppet.
- Pictures from sheets in appendices of hot and cold food.
- Pictures (or models) of fridge and cooker.
- Pencil.
- Two ring magnets.
- Three objects (one made of wood, one of metal and one of plastic).

Session 29

- Two bar magnets.
- Animal puppet.
- Large feely bag containing jacket, sock, glove, hat and scarf.
- Tambourine or shaker bells.

Chapter 30

- Tumbler, plastic box, book and a cardboard box.
- Feely bag containing a selection of transparent and opaque materials/objects.
- Torch.
- Jar containing coloured marbles.

Session 31

- Feely bag containing pictures of fur- and feather-covered creatures, and people.
- Feely bag containing inanimate objects (e.g. plastic brick, glove, spoon).
- Pencil.
- Two ring magnets.

Session 32

- Feely bag containing pictures of sense organs (nose, mouth, eyes, ears).
- Tambourine or shaker bells.

Session 33

- Feely bag containing inanimate objects (e.g. glove, spoon, ball). Include two or three pictures of animals.
- Three coloured plastic tinted sheets, one red, one yellow and one blue.
- Three objects (one made of wood, one of metal and one of plastic).

Session 34

- A push-along toy, a pull-along toy with string attached, and six cubes.
- Three coloured plastic tinted sheets, one red, one yellow and one blue.
- Pencil.
- Two ring magnets.

Session 35

- Cardboard box.
- Torch.
- Small cloth for a blanket.
- Pictures of night-time (see appendices).
- Sun shape.
- Pencil.
- Ring magnets.

Session 36

- Three objects, one made of wood, one of metal and one of plastic.
- Animal puppet.
- Jar containing coloured marbles.

Session notes

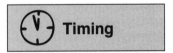

Materials

These are listed in the introduction. Most are readily available in nurseries and classrooms; others are provided as appendices.

Timing

Twenty to thirty minutes depending on the length of time spent on each game.

Key teaching points

It is essential to keep the pace of your language slow. Use 'pondering' to gain attention and interest and to slow down the pace. Also essential is keeping language as uncluttered and simple as possible.

Visual cues

Children have different learning strengths. Some learn best from hearing information, some from having it presented visually and some from activity-based tasks. Pre-school children especially learn best when all three aspects are present, and learning is substantially supported by visual materials and activities and rhythm. For this reason the sessions are designed to be active and visual with familiar rhymes. You can help the process greatly by using simple gestures to accompany descriptions and instructions.

Praise

Praise every child at least twice in each session.

Praise for good sitting before the group becomes too fidgety. Offer to sprinkle imaginary 'magic glue dust' for a child who has difficulty in sitting still.

Be positive

Try not to say, 'No, that's wrong.' Clearly there are right and wrong answers, but the group works on similar principles to brainstorming where all ideas are listened to and considered, and then an answer is chosen from all the ideas. We tend to say, 'Thank you, you spoke up really well. You gave me another idea.'

Giving time to think

When you expect a child to answer a question give him or her at least 15 seconds to respond. (You will be surprised how long that seems!) Encourage with comments such as:

> *'You are thinking really well. Well done!'*

> *'You are quiet and you are thinking about this really well!'*

If the child doesn't answer, offer support by asking:

> *'Would you like some help from us?'*

If yes, ask the group (adults included) to put up their hands if they want to help give an answer. The child then chooses someone.

Fun

Enjoy this time with the children.

Behaviour

Try, when changing the activity and the pace of the activity, to change the focus and distract from negative behaviour if it occurs. Praise the other children for behaviour that you do want to see. Try not to introduce a competitive element.

Teaching notes

The sessions outlined in this book were trialled on children in Reception year and although they seek to develop basic vocabulary needed for the Science Curriculum they also develop verbal reasoning skills.

I found in groups of 4-year-olds that initially when I asked *'How do we find out what is in the pot?'* they would tell me what was in it rather than how to find out. The use and understanding of the language of investigation and experimentation is an area we hope to have developed in this scheme. There is an emphasis on the words related to the five senses with which we explore our world.

Memory

Children are helped to recall and retain information from the sessions by several means.

- Small spirals of learning with games and activities repeated where necessary. It is important to retain this format. Some children may need sessions to be repeated two or three times if you feel they need even tighter spirals of learning.
- Use of rhyme and singing is an important way of helping children to remember information and to reproduce it later.
- For ease of use we have suggested that most songs are sung to the tune of 'Here we go round the mulberry bush' because it is familiar to most people. However, do use a different tune if you wish, but do ensure that you use the same tune each time to retain links with the idea and familiarity.
- Systematically slowing down the pace of language.
- Extensive use of visual support materials.
- Use of puppets to create an emotionally relaxed learning environment.

Remember the four Ps

Pause	to allow time to think
Pace	slow, clear and uncluttered
Ponder	to clarify questions
Praise	praise, praise, and include praise for specific behaviours

Being a mediational teacher

It is important to help young children to gain an awareness of how they learn so that they can bring conscious strategies to future learning tasks. I was reminded of this recently while attending a Brightstart course for Early Years run by Ruth Durch. The following are key pointers to moving towards mediating young children's learning in the classroom and in Spirals sessions.

- Encourage comparison, since the skill of comparing underpins the ability to categorise. Some ideas would be when doing a same/different task ask the children how many ways they differ. Use the categories (e.g. size, shape, colour).
- Encourage work on patterns. When doing a series (i.e. a pattern which follows a predictable rule), talk about what the features are and try to find the rule. Ask how the children *knew* which shape came next. How did they guess what would be next?
- When talking about a sequence of events try to establish sequential thinking by using picture clues at first which are gradually withdrawn when no longer needed.
- Every so often affirm the child but also ask: *'How did you know that or how did you do that?'* to develop conscious thinking strategies.

Plan the above into each session.

Language introduced in this book

Vocabulary introduced, then developed through the Spirals programme

Session 1	touch, ears, nose, eyes, mouth, hands, sniffing, smell, see, smooth, feel, find out
Session 2	ourselves, head, shoulders, knees, toes, senses, magnetic, shape, triangles, circles, squares, rectangles, metal, upside-down, I wonder what will happen, look, face, looking
Session 3	I looked with my, what can you see, what can I do, I can see you, I can use my eyes to, I look around, look for things, rough, what can we use to find out, how can we find out, feely fingers
Session 4	what will you use to find out, touch and explore, change, who has, magnetic shapes sticking, journey
Session 5	stuck, choose, dark, light, torch, no light, night-time, sleep
Session 6	night-time creatures, daytime creatures, wake up, surface
Session 7	see through, too
Session 8	do you remember, keep me warm, wear, clothes, why we wear these things, can you see the light, see through and not see through, cold, cool ourselves
Session 9	food we eat, hot and cold, opaque, can't see through
Session 10	what will happen
Session 11	sound
Session 12	pull, force
Session 13	push, clear or opaque
Session 14	growing things, water, light, nutrients, eat, plants, earth, food and feed, roots, suck food in, cress, clearly and muffled, push and pull, I can use my listening ears, I can hear, what can we hear
Session 16	strongest light
Session 17	it won't grow, living things, made in a factory, only living things can grow

Session 18	shake this gently and it makes a quiet sound, use more force, shake it strongly and it makes a loud sound
Session 19	what senses have we used, what did we use them for, what senses haven't we used
Session 20	what will happen, check its progress, growing, changing, longer, switch your torches on, switch your torches off
Session 21	forwards, backwards, towards, sideways, growing and not growing, properties
Session 22	happy, what force is used to make things move, fur, feather, clothes, different, move
Session 23	musical instruments, attract, repel
Session 24	changing patterns, same and different
Session 25	disappear, dissolving, dissolve, coffee
Session 26	fizzy, liquid, bicarbonate of soda
Session 27	lifted, white vinegar, colours, lines, more
Session 28	ring magnet, hover
Session 29	cheeks (different body parts), forceful, less forceful, tap, clap, listen, sound, loud, quiet
Session 30	you have power, you can light up
Session 32	help, change places
Session 33	red, yellow, blue, colour, different colour, on top, surfaces

Session 1

Materials

- Picture of nose.
- Two small covered containers (e.g. one containing bath salts, the other orange peel).
- Smooth material such as a silk scarf.
- Feely bag containing smooth and rough/coarse materials.
- Safety hand mirror.

Opening song

(Sitting)

Sit in a circle with the children. Say that you are all going to sing a new song and you will help them with the words.

Ask the group to find with their hands and touch:

Nose	ears	hand	eyes	tongue

I can touch my ears (clap twice)
I can touch my nose (clap twice)
I can touch my eyes (clap twice)
I can touch my mouth (clap twice)
And I can touch my hands (spread out fingers and wiggle them) (clap twice)

Super senses – Smell

(Sitting)

Sit down and place the picture of a nose on the carpet in the middle of the circle. Say, *'I can do something with my nose.'* Model sniffing something. Ask the children to think about what they can do with their noses. Tell them to talk to someone next to them about it.

After a minute or so bring the focus back to the circle and share their answers. If children don't give an answer say, *'You had a good think.'* Finally say, *'What can I do with my nose?'* Repeat the answer: *'Yes I can smell with my nose. Let's use our sense of smell to find out things.'*

Lay out two small covered containers containing two different scents (e.g. bath salts and orange peel). Say, *'Let's use our sense of smell to find what is in the pots.'* Model smelling the pots and your reaction to it.

Pass the first pot around the circle, commenting as each child smells it and reacts (e.g. *'Jenny is smelling the pot to find out what is in it. She looks as if she likes the smell'*).

Next, pass the second pot around and repeat the same procedure. Now ask, *'What can we use to find out what is in the pots? Talk to the person next to you'* (for half a minute).

Focus back in the circle and listen to answers (you may find that the children say what is in the pot rather than what they can use to find out what is in the pot. Focus them by repeating, *'What can we use to find out if you are right?'*).

Either combine the answers or develop them and say, *'We can use our nose to smell but we need to use our eyes to see as well.'* Uncover each pot and pass it around.

> **use pondering take your time**

Smooth surfaces

(Sitting then standing)

In the circle lay out a piece of material which is smooth (e.g. a silk scarf). Encourage the children to get up and touch the material. Say that it is smooth. Then pass it around the circle, encouraging each person to say, *'It is smooth'* by asking the question *'Is it smooth?'* Give several turns so that each child has the opportunity to choose and feel.

Encourage the children to use the words 'touch/feel' and 'rough/smooth/surface'. If a child says *'soft'*, say, *'yes, soft and smooth.'*

Smooth and not smooth

(Sitting)

Pass around a feely bag which contains smooth and rough/coarse materials. Each person takes out a piece of material and says whether it is smooth or not smooth. Encourage the use of the word 'smooth', and accept the answers the children give.

Closing round – Pass a smile in the mirror

(Standing in a circle)

Hold a mirror in front of you and smile while looking into it. Pass the mirror to the next person to do the same and so on around the circle.

Session 2

> **Materials**
> - Two pots with different scents in each.
> - Safety hand mirror.
> - Tray of magnetic shapes.

Opening Song

(Sitting/standing)

Sit in a circle. Explain that you will be singing your new song today. Practise singing together with actions:

> I can touch my ears (clap twice)
> I can touch my nose (clap twice)
> I can touch my eyes (clap twice)
> I can touch my mouth (clap twice)
> And I can touch my hands (spread out fingers and wiggle them) (clap twice).

Praise the children for precise clapping (i.e. for clapping only twice).

All stand. Say, '*We are going to sing a song about ourselves.*'
Sing the song with actions:

> Heads and shoulders knees and toes, knees and toes.
> Heads and shoulders knees and toes, knees and toes.
> Eyes and ears, and mouth and nose.
> Heads and shoulders knees and toes,
> Knees and toes.

Finding out using our senses – Smell and see

(Sitting)

Sit and point to your nose. Ponder what you can do with your nose, inviting answers from the group. Use the word *smell*.

Produce two pots containing different scents. Pass the first around once for each person to smell, then pass the second one around the circle. Ask the children, '*What can we use to find out what is in the pots?*' The group may talk about ideas in pairs. Listen to feedback after one or two minutes. Encourage the idea that we can use our noses to smell. Say, '*Yes, I use my nose to smell things and find out about them.*' Ponder what else we can use to find out.

> use
> pondering
> take your
> time

23

Next, say, *'What can we use to find out what is in the pots?'* Be prepared for the children to shout out what is in the pots rather than to say how they will do it. Just emphasise, *'Yes, but what can we use to find out what is in the pots?'*

When the children have mentioned the concept 'using their eyes' say *'Yes we can look. We can use our eyes to find out.'* Uncover the pots and pass them around one at a time to peep into the pots and answer *'What have you found out?'*

**use praise
phrases**

Magnetic shapes

(Sitting initially)

Take the tray of shapes around the circle, inviting each person to take one. Check that each child can name their shape as they take it.

Play shape basket

Say, for example, *'Triangles hand up, circles turn around, square shapes hop on one leg, rectangles touch your ears. Triangles change places, circles change places, square shapes change places, rectangles change places.'* Give each child a turn to choose a shape and change places and to encourage them to say 'change places'.

Sit back in the circle together. Place the metal tray in the middle of the circle and name and place your shape on the tray. Say, *'I want a circle on my tray, who has a circle? Kate, can you put your circle next to mine?'* Ask each person for their shape.

When all are on the tray say, *'I will turn the tray upside-down. I wonder what will happen?'* Encourage ideas.

Ponder that the shapes are not falling off the tray. Ask the group to talk in twos or threes to find reasons to explore. Listen to feedback and discuss as a group. Talk about magnetic shapes sticking to the metal tray.

**use
pondering
take your
time**

Closing round – Pass a smile in the mirror

(Standing in a circle)

Song (which will be built up over the coming sessions).

Pass a mirror:

'I look in the mirror and what do I see? I see my face looking at me.'

Session 3

Materials

- Rabbit with movable paws and eyes.
- Safety hand mirror.
- One rough and one smooth object.

Opening song

(Sitting)

Sit in a circle. Explain that you will be singing your new song today. Practise singing together with actions:

> I can touch my ears (clap twice)
> I can touch my nose (clap twice)
> I can touch my eyes (clap twice)
> I can touch my mouth (clap twice)
> And I can touch my hands (spread out fingers and wiggle them) (clap twice).

Looking at reflections

(Sitting)

Pass the mirror around the circle. Invite each person to look in the mirror and say, *'I look in the mirror and I see...'* (at first the children may only be able to say 'look' or 'see', but extend this over the following sessions).

Put away the mirror and lay out pictures of eyes, ears, nose, mouth and hands on the floor. Say, *'I looked in the mirror. I looked with my...nose'* (pick up the picture of the nose). Allow the children to correct you. Ask each child to help you by touching the appropriate symbol (eyes). As each person does this, say, *'You see with your eyes. You use your eyes to look.'*

Introduce the rabbit puppet who is covering his eyes. Say, *'"Rabbit. What can you see? Can you see the children?" 'Rabbit says, "No. I can't see anybody."'*

Ask the group to think of reasons why the rabbit can't see and to talk in pairs about this and about how they can help him to see. Listen to ideas from the pairs.

Tell the rabbit, *'Take your paws away from your eyes.'* Turn the rabbit around so he has his back to the group. He says, *'I took my paws away but I still can't see any children. What can I do?'* Encourage the children to suggest ideas to the rabbit.

Rabbit turns around and says, *'You helped me look and see. I took my paws away from my eyes, opened my eyes and turned around so that I could see you.'* He then describes some of the things around the circle.

Emphasise that the rabbit is using his sense of sight. Rabbit thanks the group for helping him to use his eyes to look well. He is carefully put away.

(It is important to treat the puppets carefully in the children's eyes to maintain their characters.)

BE POSITIVE

Action song (eyes)

(Standing)

Choose and practise an action involving your eyes (e.g. looking and winking). Walk around the circle and sing to a simple tune (e.g. 'Here we go around the mulberry bush'):

'*I can use my eyes to*... [Stop and choose an action such as]... *look around, look around, look around. I can use my eyes to look around, look around, look around, my eyes help me to see.*'

Other suggestions are:

...wink at you
...see you smile
...look for things.

> **use pondering take your time**

Is it rough?

(Sitting)

Hold an interesting rough-textured object and say, '*Is this smooth? No it is not, we call it rough.*'

Place the object in the middle of the circle and ask, '*How can we find out if it is rough or not? What can we use to find out?*' Repeat this question in exactly the same words, looking around the circle and pondering with the group. Ask the children to talk in pairs, and listen to answers about using our hands and fingers to touch and feel. Point out that you have already used your eyes to look.

Wonder aloud whether our ears could help us to find out if we listened. Finally invite the children, one by one, to test out their ideas. Encourage them to say what they will do (e.g. '*I will feel it. I will stroke it*') before they act.

Closing round – Pass the smile song

(Standing)

Ask the children to hold up their hands as if they were looking into a mirror. Then sing:

'*I look in the mirror and what do I see? I see a friendly face looking back at me. And I'm smiling, smiling. A smile makes me feel good inside. So I'm smiling, smiling and feeling good inside'.*

Session 4

Materials
- Cardboard box with a bell or other object which makes a noise.
- Rabbit with movable paws and eyes or other animal puppet with all sense organs.
- Tray of magnetic shapes.

Opening song

(Sitting)

Practise singing together with actions:

> I can touch my ears (clap twice)
> I can touch my nose (clap twice)
> I can touch my eyes (clap twice).
> I can touch my mouth (clap twice)
> And I can touch my hands and feely fingers (spread out fingers and wiggle them) (clap twice).

Add a new verse today:

> I use my ears to hear
> I use my nose to smell
> I use my eyes to see
> I use my mouth to taste
> I use my hands to feel
> **I use all my senses.**

Science detectives

(Sitting)

What is in the box? (sound, e.g. bells)

Put the box in front of you and ponder what might be in it. Say that you will ask the rabbit to help you find out. Place the pictures of the nose, eyes, ears, mouth and hands on the carpet.

Ask the rabbit, *'What can we use to find out what is in the box?'* The rabbit replies by singing this little rhyme:

> We can find out with our ears
> We can find out with our nose
> We can find out with our eyes
> We can find out with our mouths
> We can find out with our hands.

Ask, *'What will you use today? What will you use to find out what is in the box?'*

The rabbit chooses his nose. Ask the children to tell you what he can do with his nose. *'Yes. He can smell things to find out.'* The rabbit smells the box but it doesn't give him any clues.

Choose another child. Ask them to choose one of the sense-related pictures for the rabbit to use. For example, if eyes are chosen the rabbit looks at the box. Then point out that he needs to use something else to help him to open the box. If he uses his hands to open the box he can use them to feel inside. Say, *'When the rabbit has been helped to find out what is in the box pass it around for everyone to touch and explore.'*

Put away the box and the rabbit.

Magnetic shapes

(Sitting initially)

Take the tray of shapes around the circle, inviting each person to take a shape. Check that each child can name their shape as they take it.

Play shape basket

Say, for example, *'Triangles hand up, circles turn around, square shapes hop on one leg, rectangles touch your ears. Triangles change places, circles change places, square shapes change places, rectangles change places.'* Give children a turn to choose a shape and change places, and encourage them to say, *'Change places'*.

Sit back down in the circle together. Place the metal tray mid-circle and name and place your shape on the tray. Say, *'I want a circle on my tray, who has a circle? Kate, can you put your circle next to mine?'* Ask each person for their shape.

When all the shapes are on the tray, say, *'I will turn the tray upside-down. I wonder what will happen. What happened last time I did this?'* Encourage the children to remember, and use the words 'magnets', 'stuck to' and 'metal surface'.

Ponder that the shapes are not falling off the tray. Ask the group to talk in twos or threes to find reasons to explore. Listen to feedback and discuss as a group. Talk about magnetic shapes sticking to the metal tray.

> **use pondering take your time**

Walking around the circle

(Standing)

Choose an action. Practise (e.g. walking around a circle) and sing to a simple tune (e.g. 'Here we go round the mulberry bush'):

'I can use my hands to . . .' [Stop and choose an action such as] *'. . . tickle my face, tickle my face, tickle my face. I can use my hands to tickle my face on a cold and frosty morning.'*

Other suggestions:

. . . wave goodbye
. . . touch my tummy
. . . rub my nose.

Closing round – Journeys

(Standing)

Say, *'You will be making a journey across the circle. I will make my journey by jumping.'*

Demonstrate this. Encourage children to use the word 'journey' and to think of different ways of making that journey across the circle (e.g. hopping, rolling, slithering, walking).

Session 5

Materials

- Magnetic shapes.
- Tin tray.
- Wooden board.
- Large book.
- Three post-it notes and felt-tip pen to record (optional).
- Rabbit puppet (eyes covered with a scarf).
- Safety hand mirror.

Opening song

(Sitting)

Sit in a circle. Explain that you will be singing your song today. Practise singing together with actions:

> I can touch my ears (clap twice)
> I can touch my nose (clap twice)
> I can touch my eyes (clap twice)
> And I can touch my hands (spread out fingers and wiggle them) (clap twice)
> I use my ears to hear
> I use my nose to smell
> I use my eyes to see
> I use my mouth to taste
> I use my hands to feel
> **I use all my senses.**

Amazing magnets

(Sitting)

Lay out the tin tray, the wooden board and a large book. Remind the children what happened last time when the magnets stuck to one surface even when it was upside-down.

Offer around the small magnetised shapes, asking the children to say which shape they will choose before they do so. Invite each child to place their shape on to one of the surfaces. Then ponder with the group what will happen when you turn each one upside-down. Ask the children to talk in pairs for a few moments about their ideas.

Choose three children to come and sit by a board. Take ideas from the group on the first board, then ask the child to turn it upside-down, and so on to the other two. Recap that magnets stick to metal, but not to wood or paper.

Optional: say that to remember this they could place a piece of sticky paper on each surface with a tick if it sticks and an x if it does not.

30

Pass the smile song

(Standing)

Ask the children to hold up their hands as if they were looking into a mirror. Then sing:

> I look in the mirror and what do I see? I see myself looking back at me. I look in the mirror and open my eyes then I see to my surprise that I'm smiling, smiling. A smile makes you feel good inside. So I'm smiling, smiling and feeling good inside.

Looking at reflections

(Sitting)

Pass the mirror around the circle. Invite each person to look in the mirror and say, *'I look in the mirror and I see...'* (at first the children may only be able to say 'look' or 'see' but extend this over the following sessions).

Put away the mirror and lay out pictures of eyes, ears, nose, mouth and hands on the floor. Say, *'I looked in the mirror. I looked with my...ears'* (pick up the picture of the ears). Allow the children to correct you. Ask each person to help you by touching the appropriate symbol (eyes). As each person does this, say, *'You see with your eyes. You use your eyes to look.'*

Reintroduce the rabbit puppet who has a scarf over his head covering his eyes.

Say, *'Rabbit. What can you see?'*

Rabbit says, *'Nothing. I can't see anything.'*

Ask the children if they can remember what 'sense' the rabbit will need to use. Encourage talk in pairs about this. Listen to ideas from the pairs. Tell the rabbit, *'Take the scarf off your head and your eyes.'*

Rabbit says, *'You helped me look and use my sense of sight.'*
He then describes some of the things around the circle. *'I can see...'*

Encourage the children to say out loud with the rabbit, *'With our sense of sight we can see.'*

The rabbit thanks the group for helping him to use his eyes to look well. He is carefully put away.

Closing round – Journeys

(Standing)

Say, *'You will be making a journey across the circle. I will make my journey by jumping.'*

Demonstrate this. Encourage children to use the word 'journey' and to think of different ways of making that journey across the circle (e.g. hopping, rolling, slithering, walking).

End by all making a journey around the circle together.

Session 6

Materials

- Shoe box with small hole in it.
- Torch.
- Small cloth for a blanket.
- Rabbit (animal) puppet.
- Pictures of night-time (see appendices).
- Two pieces of material (one dark, one light).
- Strong-smelling substance in a covered box into which a straw is inserted.

Opening song

(Sitting)

Sit in a circle. Explain that you will be singing your song today. Practise singing together with actions:

> I can touch my ears (clap twice)
> I can touch my nose (clap twice)
> I can touch my eyes (clap twice)
> And I can touch my hands (spread out fingers and wiggle them) (clap twice)
> I use my ears to hear
> I use my nose to smell
> I use my eyes to see
> I use my mouth to taste
> I use my hands to feel
> **I use all my senses.**

Day and night

(Sitting)

Have ready a shoe box with a small hole in the side (big enough to peep into the box), and a larger hole in the top with a sliding cover.

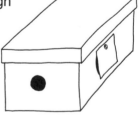

Get each child in turn to look into the box and ask them if it is light or dark inside. *'Yes, it's dark isn't it? There isn't any light getting in. But we can make it light by shining a torch into the box.'* Slide open the flap on the side of the box and shine in the torch. Let each child have another look. (Putting a small toy into the box makes the activity more interesting.)

'The box was dark. When is it dark for a long time? When we go to sleep. Night-time. It is dark at night. Perhaps you have a bedtime story – let's have one now.'

Lay out a small cloth for a blanket mid-circle.

'Little rabbit went to sleep. He thought everyone was asleep. But they weren't. Out of a corner crept Mr Fox. Mr

**use
pondering
take your
time**

Fox didn't go to sleep until very late. He crept around in the dark looking for food.'

Lay out the picture (or toy models) of Mr Fox, the owl, the dustbin, the lamp-post and the cat. Make up a story using Mr Fox and the other pictures.

Invite a child to sit in the middle of the circle and hold Mr Fox while the others tell him/her one by one to act out little scenarios.

Bring in the concepts dark and night-time, not much light to see by, sharp-eyed animals seeing in the dark. Encourage the children to talk about people they know who go to work at night.

At the end hold up a sun shape and say: *'The sun came up slowly and all the night creatures went home to bed and people and daytime creatures started to wake up.'*

BE
POSITIVE

Light and dark surfaces

(Sitting then standing)

Lay out two pieces of material in the middle of the circle, one light and one dark (e.g. a sheet of white paper and a sheet of dark coloured paper). Encourage children to take turns to choose which they will touch. Encourage children to say *'light'* or *'dark'* before they get up to touch the surface of their choice. Give several turns so that each child has the opportunity to choose and feel both materials.

Ponder with the children the different use of the word 'light' as in describing weight or appearance. *'We say something is "light" when it isn't heavy.'*

All stand and ask a child, *'Will you stand on the light surface or the dark surface?'*

When the child has had a turn ask them to choose someone else to take a turn. That person is then invited to choose someone else, and so on until everyone has taken a turn.

Smell without seeing

(Sitting)

Insert a straw into the covered box containing a strong-smelling substance and pass the box round. Encourage the children to use their noses to smell and try to identify what is in the container. Then talk in pairs to share ideas. See if they can guess what it is.

Again in pairs talk about checking: how can we check if we are right?

'We used our noses to find out. Now what can we use? Yes, we can look with our eyes.'

Remove the lid and pass the container around the circle.

Closing round – Pass the smile song

(Standing)

Ask the children to hold up their hands as if they were looking into a mirror. Then sing:

I look in the mirror and what do I see? I see myself looking back at me. I look in the mirror and open my eyes then I see to my surprise that I'm smiling, smiling. A smile makes you feel good inside. So I'm smiling, smiling and feeling good inside.

Session 7

Materials
- Three different fish shapes cut out from transparent material.
- Torch.
- Tray of magnetic shapes.
- Small cloth for a blanket.
- Pictures of night-time (see appendices).

Opening Song

(Sitting)

Sit in a circle. Explain that you will be singing your song today. Practise singing together with actions:

> I can touch my ears (clap twice)
> I can touch my nose (clap twice)
> I can touch my eyes (clap twice)
> And I can touch my hands (spread out fingers and wiggle them) (clap twice)
> I use my ears to hear
> I use my nose to smell
> I use my eyes to see
> I use my mouth to taste
> I use my hands to feel
> **I use all my senses**.

See-through fish

(Sitting in a circle)

In the middle of the circle place three different fish shapes made out of transparent material. Show the children a torch.

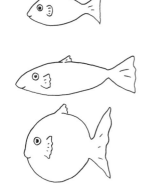

Ask, *'When I switch a torch on what will happen?'* Encourage responses which indicate that it will give light.

Say, *'Sometimes light will shine through things and you can see it on the other side.'* Choose a child and give them the torch. Ask them, *'Can you see the light?'* Invite the child to pick up one of the material squares and hold the torch behind it. They can all look to see if the material will let the light through. Ask the child to choose another child to take a turn, and repeat until everyone has had a go.

Sing a little song (to the tune of 'Here we go round the mulberry bush'):

> This is a see-through fish, a see-through fish, a see-through fish.
> This is a see-through fish, we can see the light through it.

Magnetic attraction

(Standing)

Pass around the tray of magnets and invite each person to take a shape. Encourage each person to say what shape they have chosen. Say, for example, *'I have a red square and I want a pink square too.'* Model going around the circle to see how many magnets will stick to yours.

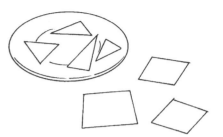

Day and night

(Sitting)

Last time we looked into the box we couldn't see very much. Ponder why. It was dark. *'The light couldn't get into the box. What did we do? We used a torch to give us light. When we turned it off it was dark in the box.'*

Ponder that dark happens when there is no light. *'The box was dark for a little while. When is it dark for a long time? When we go to sleep. Night-time. It is dark at night. What do we do? Let us hear a night-time story.'*

Lay out a small cloth for a blanket in the middle circle.

'Little rabbit went to sleep. He thought everyone was asleep. But they weren't. Out of a corner crept Mr Fox. Mr Fox didn't go to sleep until very late. He crept around in the dark looking for food.'

Lay out the picture or models of Mr Fox, the owl, the dustbin, the lamp-post and the cat. Make up a story using Mr Fox and the other pictures. Then invite a child to sit in the middle of the circle and hold Mr Fox while the others tell him/her one by one to act out little scenarios.

Bring in the concepts of dark and night-time, not much light to see by, sharp-eyed animals seeing in the dark. Encourage the children to talk about people they know who go to work at night.

At the end hold up a sun shape and say the sun came up slowly and all the night creatures went home to bed while people and daytime creatures started to wake up.

Closing round – Journeys

(Standing)

Say, *'We will be making a journey across the circle. I will make my journey by jumping.'*

Demonstrate this. Encourage children to use the word 'journey' and to think of different ways of making that journey across the circle (e.g. hopping, rolling, slithering, walking).

End by making a journey together.

use praise phrases

Session 8

Materials

- Animal puppet.
- Feely bag.
- Jacket, sock, tie, scarf.
- Three different transparent fish shapes.
- One (opaque) fish shape.
- Torch.

Opening song

(Sitting)

Sit in a circle. Explain that you will be singing your song today. Practise singing together with actions:

I can touch my ears (clap twice)
I can touch my nose (clap twice)
I can touch my eyes (clap twice)
And I can touch my hands (spread out fingers and wiggle them)
(clap twice)
I use my ears to hear
I use my nose to smell
I use my eyes to see
I use my mouth to taste
I use my hands to feel
I use all my senses.

Then say, *'I have five senses. Count them out on your fingers. I hear, I smell, I see, I taste, I feel.'*

Ask the children to hold up their hands as if they were looking into a mirror. Then sing:

I look in the mirror and what do I see?
I see myself looking back at me.
I look in the mirror and open my eyes then I see to my surprise that I'm smiling, smiling. A smile makes you feel good inside. So I'm smiling, smiling and feeling good inside.

Keep me warm (clothes)

(Sitting)

The science rabbit says that he doesn't get very cold because he is wearing something warm. The children have to guess what it is. The little animal says, *'Yes, I've got fur to keep me warm.'* He then asks the children to talk in pairs about what they wear to keep warm.

Take the following items out of a large feely bag, asking each time, '*Would we wear this to keep warm?*':

A jacket   a sock   a glove   a hat   a scarf

Talk about why you would wear these clothes.

BE POSITIVE

See-through fish

(Sitting in a circle)

In the middle of a circle place three different fish shapes made out of transparent material, and one not see-through (opaque).

| use
pondering
take your
time |

Say, '*Sometimes light will shine through things and you can see it on the other side.*' Choose a child and give them the torch. Ask them, '*Can you see the light?*' Then invite them to pick up one of the fish and hold the torch behind it, then all look to see if it will let the light through. Ask the child to choose another child to take a turn and repeat until everyone has had a go.

Talk about shapes being 'see-through' or not 'see-through'.

Ask the children to hold out the see-through fish shapes and then sing a little song (to the tune of 'Here we go round the mulberry bush'):

> These are the see-through fish, the see-through fish, the
>   see-through fish.
> These are see-through fish, we can see the light through
>   them.

Closing round – Warm and cold

(Standing)

Ask the children to suggest ideas about what they would do if they were cold (e.g. rub their hands, rub their arms, shiver, jump up and down to keep warm). Combine this into a song to the tune of '*This is the way we keep ourselves warm, this is the way we keep ourselves warm on a cold and frosty morning*'.

Talk about things you do when you are warm (e.g. fan your face, splash your face with water, lick ice-creams). Combine this into a song to the tune of '*This is the way we cool ourselves down, this is the way we cool ourselves down on a hot and sunny morning*'.

Session 9

Materials

- Animal puppet.
- Pictures or real examples of hot and cold food.
- Safety hand mirror.
- Rabbit puppet with scarf over eyes.
- Four pieces of opaque material cut into the shape of a snake.
- Torch.

Opening Song

(Sitting)

Sit in a circle. Explain that you will be singing your song today. Practise singing together with actions:

> I can touch my ears (clap twice)
> I can touch my nose (clap twice)
> I can touch my eyes (clap twice)
> And I can touch my hands (spread out fingers and wiggle them) (clap twice)
> I use my ears to hear
> I use my nose to smell
> I use my eyes to see
> I use my mouth to taste
> I use my hands to feel
> **I use all my senses.**

Then say, *'I have five senses. Count them out on your fingers. I hear, I smell, I see, I taste, I feel.'*

Warm and cold

(Standing)

Ask the children to suggest ideas about what they would do if they were cold (e.g. rub their hands, rub their arms, shiver, jump up and down to keep warm). Combine this into a song to the tune of *'This is the way we keep ourselves warm, this is the way we keep ourselves warm on a cold and frosty morning'*.

Talk about things you do when you are warm (e.g. fan your face, splash your face with water, lick ice-creams). Combine this into a song to the tune of *'This is the way we cool ourselves down, this is the way we cool ourselves down on a hot and sunny morning'*.

Keeping warm (food and drink)

(Sitting)

The little animal puppet reminds the children that last time they looked at how clothes kept them warm. Encourage the children to use the words – 'clothes keep us warm' – and encourage them to remember what clothes they looked at in the last session. This time they will be looking at food we eat when we are hot and food we eat when we are cold.

Lay out pictures of hot drinks, hot food, ice-cream, a drink containing ice-cubes, and jelly. Ask the children to talk in pairs about which they would eat when they are hot. Listen to ideas, then talk about the warming food and drinks.

Looking at reflections

(Sitting)

Pass the mirror around the circle. Invite each person to look in the mirror and say, *'I look in the mirror and I see…'* (at first the children may only be able to say 'look' or 'see' but extend this over the following sessions).

Put away the mirror and lay out pictures of eyes, ears, nose, mouth and hands on the floor, and say, *'I looked in the mirror. I looked with my…ears'* (pick up the picture of the ears).

Allow the children to correct you. Ask each person to help you by touching the appropriate symbol (eyes). As each person does this, say, *'You see with your eyes. You use your eyes to look.'*

Reintroduce the rabbit puppet who has a scarf over his head covering his eyes. Say, *'Rabbit. What can you see?'* Rabbit says, *'Nothing. I can't see anything.'*

Ask the children if they can remember what 'sense' the rabbit will need to use. Encourage talk in pairs about this. Listen to ideas from the pairs.

Tell the rabbit, *'Take your scarf off your head and your eyes.'* He then ponders, *'That is my sense of sight.'*

He then describes some of the things around the circle. *'I can see. …'* Encourage the children to say out loud with the rabbit, *'With our sense of sight we can see.'*

> **use pondering take your time**

Rabbit thanks the group for helping him to use his eyes to look well. He is carefully put away.

Opaque snake

(Sitting in a circle)

Lay out four pieces of opaque material cut in the shape of a snake. Invite the children, as before, to shine the torch, holding it behind the material to spot if they can see the light through the other side. Say that there is a special word for things

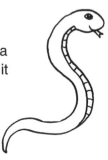

that don't let light through. This word is 'opaque'. Sing a little song to the tune of 'Here we go round the mulberry bush', holding a snake shape:

I am the opaque snake, opaque snake, opaque snake,
I am the opaque snake, you can't see through me.

Closing round – Pass the smile song

(Standing)

Ask the children to hold up their hands as if they were looking into a mirror. Then sing:

I look in the mirror and what do I see? I see myself looking back at me. I look in the mirror and open my eyes, then I see to my surprise that I'm smiling, smiling. A smile makes you feel good inside. So I'm smiling, smiling and feeling good inside.

Session 10

> ## Materials
> - Magnetic shapes.
> - Tin tray.
> - Wooden board.
> - Large book.
> - Post-it notes and a pen to record (optional).
> - Feely bag containing an unusually shaped solid object.
> - Torch.
> - Four pieces of material cut into the shape of a snake.

Opening Song

(Sitting)

Sit in a circle. Explain that you will be singing a song today. Practise singing together with actions:

> I can touch my ears (clap twice)
> I can touch my nose (clap twice)
> I can touch my eyes (clap twice)
> And I can touch my hands (spread out fingers and wiggle them) (clap twice)
> I use my ears to hear
> I use my nose to smell
> I use my eyes to see
> I use my mouth to taste
> I use my hands to feel
> **I use all my senses.**

Encourage the children to count on their fingers the five senses, saying: *'I hear, I smell, I see, I taste, I feel.'*

Amazing magnets

(Sitting)

Lay out the tin tray, the wooden board and the large book. Remind the children what happened last time when the magnets stuck to one surface even when it was upside-down.

Offer around the small magnetised shapes, asking the children to say which shape they will choose before they do so. Invite the children to place their shapes on to one of the surfaces.

Ponder with the group what will happen when you turn each surface upside-down. Ask children to talk in pairs for a few moments about their ideas.

Choose three children to each come and sit by tray/board/book. Take ideas from the group by the first board then ask the child to turn it upside-down, and so on to the other two.

Recap that magnets stick to the metal but not to the wood or paper.

Say that to remember it we could put a piece of sticky paper on each surface with a tick if it sticks and an x if it does not.

Shadow puppets

(Sitting)

Pass around a feely bag containing a solid object and invite the children to use their 'feely fingers' to feel the object but they must not look. Tell them that they will really want to look but not to do so until everyone has had a turn.

Then take the object out of the bag and place it in the middle of the circle. Invite the children to shine the torch on to it to see what the shadow will look like.

Opaque snake

(Sitting in a circle)

Lay out four pieces of opaque material cut in the shape of a snake. Invite the children, as before, to shine the torch and to hold it against the material and see if they can see the light through the other side. Ask first whether they will see the light through it. Say that there is a special word for things that don't let light through. This word is 'opaque'. Sing a little song to the tune of 'Here we go round the mulberry bush' while passing the snake shape around the circle:

I am the opaque snake, opaque snake, opaque snake,
I am the opaque snake, you can't see through me.

Closing round – Warm and cold

(Standing)

Ask the children to suggest ideas about what they would do if they were cold (e.g. rub their hands, rub their arms, shiver, jump up and down to keep warm). Combine this into a song to the tune of 'Here we go round the mulberry bush': *'This is the way we keep ourselves warm, this is the way we keep ourselves warm on a cold and frosty morning.'*

Talk about things you do when you are hot (e.g. fan your face, splash your face with water, lick ice-creams).

Session 11

Materials

- Pictures of night-time (see appendices).
- Picture of types of people who work at night.
- Instruments played by shaking them.
- Animal puppet.
- Pictures or real examples of hot and cold food.
- Pictures (or models) of a fridge and a cooker.
- Small cloth.

Opening song

(Sitting)

Sit in a circle. Explain that you will be singing your song today. Practise singing together with actions:

> I can touch my ears (clap twice)
> I can touch my nose (clap twice)
> I can touch my eyes (clap twice)
> And I can touch my hands (spread out fingers and wiggle them) (clap twice)
> I use my ears to hear
> I use my nose to smell
> I use my eyes to see
> I use my mouth to taste
> I use my hands to feel
> **I use all my senses.**

Encourage the children to count on their fingers the five senses, saying, *'I hear, I smell, I see, I taste, I feel.'*

BE
POSITIVE

Day and night

(Sitting)

'*Last time we looked into the box and couldn't see very much.*' Ponder why. '*It was dark. The light couldn't get into the box. What did we do? We used a torch to give us light. When we turned it off it was dark in the box.*'

Ponder that dark happens when there is no light. '*The box was dark for a little while. When is it dark for a long time? When we go to sleep. Night-time. It is dark at night. What do we do? Let us hear a night-time story.*'

Lay out a small cloth for a blanket in the middle of the circle.

'*Little rabbit went to sleep. He thought everyone was asleep. But they weren't. Out of a corner crept Mr Fox. Mr Fox didn't go to sleep until very late. He crept around in the dark looking for food.*'

Use the night-time picture from the appendices – or a fox puppet – and make up a story about night-time creatures, asking the children for ideas as you go along (e.g. It was a dark night and the fox was.............. What do you think he was doing?) Bring in the concepts dark and night-time, not much light to see by, sharp-eyed animals seeing in the dark. Encourage the children to talk about people they know who go to work at night.

At the end hold up a sun shape and say the sun came up slowly and all the night creatures went home to bed while people and daytime creatures started to wake up.

Chase the sound maker

(Standing)

One child stands in the middle with their eyes closed. Give a (shaken) instrument to another child and ask them all to stand in a circle around the first child, with their hands behind their backs. Tell the child in the middle to find out who is holding the sound maker.

Ask the child to open their eyes. The game is to ask a person in the circle, *'Have you got the sound maker?'* If they have they must shake it behind their back. Once the seeker is sure, they say, *'You have the sound maker.'* If they are wrong then they keep guessing until they have chosen the right person. Take turns around the circle several times to encourage listening skills and the use of vocabulary.

Keeping warm (food and drink)

(Sitting)

The little animal puppet reminds the children that last time they looked at how clothes kept them warm. Encourage the children to use the words 'clothes keep us warm', and encourage them to remember what clothes they looked at during the previous session. This time they will be looking at food we eat when we are hot and food we eat when we are cold.

Lay out pictures of hot and cold food and drink. Ask the children to talk in pairs about trying to remember which foods were hot (warming foods) and which were cold (cooling foods).

Lay out on one side of the circle a picture of a fridge and on the other side a picture of a cooker. Ask the children to put the food and drink in the correct place (by the cooker or by the fridge). Once this has been done, ponder what the cooker does to make the food or drink hot. Listen to ideas about other food and drink they can think of which are hot or cold.

Closing round – Journeys in the dark

(Standing)

Say, *'You will be making a journey across the circle. You will pretend it is night-time and you can't see very well in the dark because there isn't much light. I will make my journey by jumping.'*

Demonstrate this. Ask the children to move across the circle carefully, using a pretend torch to light the way. Encourage them to use the word 'journey' and to think of different ways of making that journey across the circle (e.g. creeping, walking, tiptoeing).

End by making a journey together.

relax and
have fun

Session 12

Materials

- Tambourine and shaker bells.
- Three pull-along toys (these could include a large plastic or cardboard box).
- Pictures (or models) of a fridge and a cooker.
- Feely bag containing an unusually shaped solid object.
- Torch.

Sounds like this

(Sitting)

We are going to look at some musical instruments. They are things that make music. Lay out some instruments (e.g. a tambourine, some shaker bells). In pairs, talk about how you would play these instruments. Pass the tambourine around for the children to share their ideas; then pass the second instrument around. Say that you are going to choose two children to play them as you all sing the opening song.

Opening song

(Sitting)

Sit in a circle. Explain that you will be singing your song today. Practise singing together with actions:

> I can touch my ears (clap twice)
> I can touch my nose (clap twice)
> I can touch my eyes (clap twice)
> And I can touch my hands (spread out fingers and wiggle them) (clap twice)
> I use my ears to hear
> I use my nose to smell
> I use my eyes to see
> I use my mouth to taste
> I use my hands to feel
> **I use all my senses.**

Encourage the children to count on their fingers the five senses, saying, *'I hear, I smell, I see, I taste, I feel.'*

BE
POSITIVE

Chase the sound maker

(Standing)

One child stands in the middle with their eyes closed. Give an instrument to one of the children and ask all the children to stand with their hands behind their backs. Tell the child in the middle to find out who is holding the sound maker.

Ask the child to open their eyes. The game is to ask a person in the circle, *'Have you got the sound maker?'* If they have they must shake it behind their back.

When the seeker is sure, they say, *'You have the sound maker.'*

If they are wrong then they keep guessing until they have chosen the right person. Take turns around the circle several times to encourage listening skills and the use of vocabulary.

Pull (force)

(Sitting)

Lay out three items – all pull-along toys with string attached. These could include a large plastic or cardboard box. Ask the children for their ideas on what the toys are and what you would do with them. Say, *'If you want to make a toy move you have to use "a force". That is what we call it when we move something.'*

Ask each person in the group to choose one of the toys to pull. Use the words, *'I will pull the string/the toy.'*

Review – What senses have I used?

Remind the children what the senses are and what we use them for. Ask the children in pairs to think about what senses they have used and listen to feedback. Emphasise – eyes to look and see, ears to hear the instruments, hands to touch and feel. Ask what senses you haven't used.

Shadow puppets

(Sitting)

Pass a feely bag containing a solid object around the circle and invite the children to use their feely fingers to feel the object, but that they must not look. Tell them that they will really want to look, but not to do so until everyone has had a turn.

Then take the object out of the bag. Put it in the middle of the circle. Invite the children to shine the torch on to it to see what the shadow will look like.

> **use
> pondering
> take your
> time**

48

Closing round – Journeys in the light

(Standing)

Say, *'You will be making a journey across the circle. You will pretend it is daytime and you can see very well because there is a lot of light. I will make my journey by jumping.'*

Ask the children where the light is coming from. Ask them to move across the circle by creeping, then walking, then tiptoeing.

End by making a journey together.

Session 13

Sounds like this

(Sitting)

Say, *'We are going to look at some musical instruments. They are things that make music.'*

Lay out some instruments (e.g. a tambourine), and a different instrument from last time (e.g. a whistle or a flute). In pairs, talk about how you would play these instruments. Pass the tambourine around for the children to share their ideas; then pass the second instrument around. Say that you are going to choose two children to play the instruments while you all sing the opening song.

Opening song

(Sitting)

Sit in a circle. Explain that you will be singing your song today. Practise singing together with actions:

I can touch my ears (clap twice)
I can touch my nose (clap twice)
I can touch my eyes (clap twice)
And I can touch my hands (spread out fingers and wiggle them) (clap twice)
I use my ears to hear
I use my nose to smell
I use my eyes to see
I use my mouth to taste
I use my hands to feel
I use all my senses.

Encourage the children to count on their fingers the five senses, saying, *'I hear, I smell, I see, I taste, I feel.'*

Chase the sound maker

(Standing)

One child stands in the middle with their eyes closed. Give a (shaken) instrument to one of the children and ask all the children to stand with their hands behind their backs. Tell the child in the middle that they will have to find out who is holding the sound maker.

Ask the child to open their eyes. The game is to ask a person in the circle, *'Have you got the sound maker?'* If they have, they must shake it behind their back. When the seeker is sure, then they say, *'You have the sound maker'.* If they are wrong, then they must keep guessing until they have chosen the right person. Take turns around the circle several times to encourage the listening skills and the use of vocabulary.

use praise phrases

See-through fish and opaque snake

(Sitting in a circle)

Lay out a selection of clear fish shapes and opaque snake shapes. Say to the children, *'Here is the torch, choose a shape to shine on it. Choose either the opaque snake or the see-through fish.'*

Ensure that the children use the words 'see-through' and 'opaque'. Give each person in the circle a turn. You can ask the children to choose the next person for their turn.

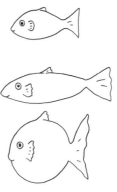

Push (force)

(Sitting)

Lay out three push-along items (these could include a large plastic or cardboard box). Ask the children for their ideas on what the toys are and what you would do with them. Say, *'If you want to make a toy move you have to use "a force". That is what we call it when we move something.'* Ask each person in the group to choose one of the toys to push. Use the words, *'I will push the toy.'*

Closing round – Pass the smile song

(Standing)

Ask the children to hold up their hands as if they were looking into a mirror. Then sing:

I look in the mirror and what do I see?
I see a friendly face looking back at me.
And I'm smiling, smiling. A smile makes me
feel good inside. So I'm smiling, smiling and
feeling good inside.

relax and have fun

Session 14

> **Materials**
> - Something that will grow (e.g. cress seeds).
> - Pictures of water, sun and items of food.
> - Tambourine and bag made of thick material.
> - Three items: a push-along toy, a pull-along toy with string attached and a large plastic or cardboard box.

Opening Song

(Sitting)

Sit in a circle. Explain that you will be singing your song today. Practise singing together with actions:

> I can touch my ears (clap twice)
> I can touch my nose (clap twice)
> I can touch my eyes (clap twice)
> And I can touch my hands (spread out fingers and wiggle them) (clap twice)
> I use my ears to hear
> I use my nose to smell
> I use my eyes to see
> I use my mouth to taste
> I use my hands to feel
> **I use all my senses.**

Encourage the children to count on their fingers the five senses, saying, *'I hear, I smell, I see, I taste, I feel.'*

Growing things – What do we need?

(Sitting)

Show the children some cress seeds and say, *'These are very little cress seeds. If we put them in the earth and give them water and light, they will grow. We need three main things to help them to grow – water, light and nutrients.'*

Show them pictures of water and the sun. Adopt a puzzled air: *'Nutrients, what are nutrients?'* Say that you will ask the science rabbit. Bring out the rabbit and ask him a question: *'Growing things need water [point to the picture] and light [point to the picture], and they need nutrients, but what does that mean?'*

The rabbit explains: *'Ah, nutrients are the things that feed us. I feed on grass and vegetables. Children eat different things. Children, what do you eat to give you nutrients?'*

Ask the children to reply. Then say, *'Plants need food too, but they can't eat chips and beans and ice-creams which you like to eat.*

They get theirs from the earth and special ones in water.'

Say, *'So, we get nutrients from the things we feed on. But plants don't have mouths or teeth.'*

The rabbit replies, *'That is true, they use their roots instead to suck food in.'*

use
pondering
take your
time

Show the children some cress seeds and a carton of grown cress. The grown cress has had light, water and nutrients to make it grow. Grow several at a time so that you have a substitute if one fails. Encourage the children to try this at home with their parents' help.

Clear sound and muffled sound

(Standing and sitting)

Stand in a circle. Give a tambourine to the person next to you to shake. Invite them to shake it, then to walk across the circle to give it to someone else to shake until everyone has had a turn.

Sit down. Introduce a bag made of thick material. Ask the children to talk in pairs as you put the tambourine into the bag and shake it again. Ask, *'Will I hear it clearly?'* Listen to ideas. Place the tambourine in the bag. All stand up. Pass the tambourine in the bag around the circle to allow each person to have a shake.

When everyone has had a turn, ask, *'Could you hear it as clearly or was it muffled?'* Talk about it being muffled.

Take the tambourine out of the bag and pass it around for a final shake.

relax and
have fun

Push and pull (force)

(Sitting)

Lay out three items: a push-along toy, a pull-along toy with string attached, and a large plastic or cardboard box. Ask the children for their ideas on what the toys are and what you would do with them. Say, *'If you want to make a toy move you have to use "a force". That is what we call it when we push or pull something.'* Ask each person in the group which force they will use – push or pull – and then choose a toy to do this. Encourage use of the words 'push' and 'pull' (e.g. 'I will push the toy', 'I will pull the string'). When everybody has taken a turn, invite ideas as to what you could do to move the box.

Encourage use of the words 'forwards', 'backwards', 'towards' and 'sideways' as in 'Push the box forwards, pull the box backwards and towards John'.

Closing round – The listening song

(Standing)

To the tune of 'Here we go round the mulberry bush':

I can use my listening ears, listening ears, listening ears,
I can use my listening ears and I can hear a bee [All buzz].

I can use my listening ears, listening ears, listening ears,
I can use my listening ears and I can hear a cow [All moo].

I can use my listening ears, listening ears, listening ears,
I can use my listening ears and I can hear . . . [STOP] What can we hear?

Encourage the children to tell you what they can hear.

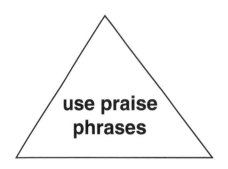

Session 15

```
                    Materials
 • Tambourine.
 • Percussion instrument (e.g. drum).
 • See-through fish and opaque snake.
 • Cress seeds to check for growth.
 • Torch.
```

Sounds like this

(Sitting)

Say, *'We are going to look at some musical instruments. They are things that make music.'*

Lay out some instruments (e.g. a tambourine), and a different instrument from last time (e.g. a drum kit). In pairs, talk about how you would play these. Pass the tambourine around for the children to share their ideas, then pass the second instrument around.

Say that you are going to choose two children to play them as you all sing the opening song.

Opening song

(Sitting)

Sit in a circle. Explain that you will be singing your song today. Practise singing together with actions:

> I can touch my ears (clap twice)
> I can touch my nose (clap twice)
> I can touch my eyes (clap twice)
> And I can touch my hands (spread out fingers and wiggle them) (clap twice)
> I use my ears to hear
> I use my nose to smell
> I use my eyes to see
> I use my mouth to taste
> I use my hands to feel
> **I use all my senses.**

Encourage the children to count on their fingers the five senses, saying, *'I hear, I smell, I see, I taste, I feel.'*

Growing things – What do we need?

(Standing)

Ask the children to talk in pairs to see if they remember what growing things need. Bring in the science rabbit and the 'growing' picture from the appendices. Encourage the children to say what seeds need to grow. Check the cress seeds for progress. Ask if they are changing and comment as necessary. Encourage the words 'growing', 'changing' and 'longer'.

use
pondering
take your
time

Chase the sound maker

(Standing)

One child stands in the middle with their eyes closed. Tell them they will have to find out who is holding the sound maker and what they are making the sound with.

Give the two instruments to two of the children. Point to one child to show that you want them to make a sound with their instrument and then the other child takes their turn. The child in the middle opens their eyes and says what the instrument was and who made the noise. They close their eyes again and repeat the process with the other child with the sound maker. Then they open their eyes.

The game is to ask a person in the circle: *'Have you got the sound maker?'* If they have it, they must shake it behind their back. When the seeker is sure, they say, *'You have the sound maker.'*

If they are wrong they must keep guessing until they have chosen the right person. Take turns around the circle several times to encourage listening skills and the use of vocabulary.

BE
POSITIVE

See-through fish and opaque snake

(Sitting)

Lay out a selection of clear fish shapes and opaque snake shapes. Say to the children, *'Here is the torch. Will you shine it on the opaque snake or the see-through fish?'* Ensure that children use the words 'see-through' and 'opaque'. Give each person in the circle a turn. You can ask the children to choose the next person for their turn.

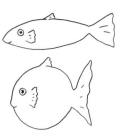

Closing game – Journeys in the light

(Standing)

Say, *'You will be making a journey across the circle. You will pretend it is daytime and you can see very well because there is a lot of light. I will make my journey by jumping.'*

Ask the children where the light is coming from. Ask the children to move across the circle by creeping, then walking, then tiptoeing.

Session 16

```
┌─────────────────────────────────────────────────────────────┐
│                         Materials                           │
│  •  Cress seeds to check for growth.                        │
│  •  Top up water.                                           │
│  •  Dark box.                                               │
│  •  Small cloth for a blanket.                              │
│  •  Pictures of night-time.                                 │
│  •  Picture of types of people who work at night and their vehicles. │
│  •  Shaker bells and bag made of thick material.            │
└─────────────────────────────────────────────────────────────┘
```

Opening song

(Sitting)

Sit in a circle. Explain that you will be singing your song today. Practise singing together with actions:

> I can touch my ears (clap twice)
> I can touch my nose (clap twice)
> I can touch my eyes (clap twice)
> And I can touch my hands (spread out fingers and wiggle them) (clap twice)
> I use my ears to hear
> I use my nose to smell
> I use my eyes to see
> I use my mouth to taste
> I use my hands to feel
> **I use all my senses.**

Encourage the children to count on their fingers the five senses, saying, *'I hear, I smell, I see, I taste, I feel.'*

Growing things – What do we need?

(Standing)

Ask the children to talk in pairs to see if they remember what growing things need. Bring in the science rabbit and the 'growing' picture. Check the cress seeds for progress. Ask if they are changing and comment as necessary. Encourage the words 'growing', 'changing' and 'longer'.

Day and night

(Sitting)

Say, *'Last time we looked into the box we couldn't see very much.'* Ponder why. *'It was dark. The light couldn't get into the box. What did we do? We used a torch to give us light. When we turned it off it was dark in the box.'*

Ponder that dark happens when there is no light. *'The box was dark for a little while. When is it dark for a long time? When we go to sleep. Night-time. It is dark at night. What do we do? Let's hear a night-time story.'*

use
pondering
take your
time

Lay out a small cloth for a blanket in the middle of the circle. *'Little rabbit went to sleep. He thought everyone was asleep. But they weren't. Out of a corner crept Mr Fox. Mr Fox didn't go to sleep until very late. He crept around in the dark looking for food.'*

Make up a story using Mr Fox then invite the children to suggest what might happen.

Bring in the concepts of dark and night-time, not much light to see by, sharp-eyed animals seeing in the dark.

Encourage the children to talk about people they know who go to work at night. *'Why isn't it dark in the daytime?'*

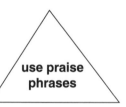

Talk about the sun being the strongest light. Talk about it being a very strong light and the dangers of looking straight at it, and that we should not look straight at it.

At the end, hold up a sun shape and say, *'The sun came up slowly and all the night creatures went home to bed, and people and daytime creatures started to wake up.'*

Clear sound and muffled sound

(Standing)

Standing in a circle, take a different instrument from last time (e.g. shaker bells). Ask the children how we play the instrument and give it a shake so that the children hear the bells. Talk about the force needed to make a noise (e.g. a gentle shake = a quiet sound and a strong shake = a loud sound).

Pass it to the person next to you. Invite them to shake it, then to walk across the circle and give it to someone else to shake until everyone has had a turn.

Sit down. Introduce a bag made of a thick material. Ask the children to talk in pairs as you place the shaker bells into the bag and shake it again. Ask, *'Will I hear it clearly?'*

Listen to ideas. Place the shaker bells into the bag. All stand. Pass the shaker bells in the bag around the circle to allow each person to have a shake. When everyone has had a turn, ask, *'Could you hear it as clearly or was it muffled?'*

use praise
phrases

Talk about it being muffled. Take the shaker bells out of the bag and pass the instrument around for a final shake.

Closing round – Torches on and torches off

(Standing)

Tell the children that they will pretend to be torches. When you say, *'Switch your torches on'* they will open their eyes; when you say, *'Switch your torches off'* they will close their eyes.

Practise this as a group.

relax and
have fun

Session 17

Materials

- Cress seeds to check for growth.
- Top up water.
- Tambourine and triangle or wooden beater.
- Animal puppet.
- Plastic cube.
- Science rabbit.
- See-through fish and opaque snake.
- Torch.

Sounds like this

(Sitting)

Say, *'We are going to look at some musical instruments. They are things that make music.'* Lay out an instrument (e.g. a tambourine), and a different instrument from last time (e.g. a triangle or a wooden beater). In pairs, talk about how you would play these instruments. Pass the tambourine around for the children to share their ideas, then pass the second instrument around. Say that you are going to choose two children to play them as you all sing the opening song.

Opening song

(Sitting)

Sit in a circle. Explain that you will be singing your song today. Practise singing together with actions:

> I can touch my ears (clap twice)
> I can touch my nose (clap twice)
> I can touch my eyes (clap twice)
> And I can touch my hands (spread out fingers and wiggle them) (clap twice)
> I use my ears to hear
> I use my nose to smell
> I use my eyes to see
> I use my mouth to taste
> I use my hands to feel
> **I use all my senses.**

Encourage the children to count on their fingers the five senses, saying, *'I hear, I smell, I see, I taste, I feel.'*

Growing things – What do we need?

(Standing)

Ask the children to talk in pairs to see if they remember what growing things need. Bring in the science rabbit and the 'growing' picture. Check the cress seeds for progress. Ask if they are changing and comment as necessary. Use the words 'growing', 'changing' and 'bigger'.

Introduce an animal puppet who brings along a plastic cube. He says, *'I want to give my cube light and water and nutrients to make it grow bigger so that I can stand on it.'* The science rabbit says, 'It won't grow.'

The little animal asks the children, *'Why won't it grow?'* Explore reasons, then appeal to the science rabbit. The science rabbit says, *'Only living things can grow. This isn't a living thing. It's made in a factory.'*

The animal asks, *'What is a factory?'* The rabbit replies, '*It's a place where people make things.'*

> **use**
> **pondering**
> **take your**
> **time**

The little animal says, *'I don't believe you. I'm going to give my cube water, light and nutrients and see if it will grow'.* Put the cube in a dish of water in the light beside the cress seeds. Ask the children to tell you what they think will happen.

Chase the sound maker

(Standing)

One child stands in the middle with their eyes shut. Give a (shaken) instrument to one of the children and ask them all to stand with their hands behind their backs.

Tell the child in the middle, *'You have to find out who is holding the sound maker.'* Ask them to open their eyes. The game is to ask someone in the circle, *'Have you got the sound maker?'* If they have they must shake it behind their back.

BE POSITIVE

When the seeker is sure, then they say, *'You have the sound maker.'* If they are wrong they must keep guessing until they have chosen the right person. Take turns around the circle several times to encourage listening skills and the use of vocabulary.

See-through fish and opaque snake

(Sitting in a circle)

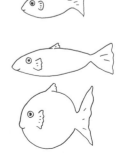

Lay out a selection of clear fish shapes and opaque snake shapes. Say to the children, *'Here is the torch. Shine it on to the opaque snake or the see-through fish.'* Ensure that the children use the words 'see-through' and 'opaque'. Give each person in the circle a turn. You can ask the children to choose the next person for their turn.

Closing round – Changing journeys

(Standing)

Say to the children, *'Choose how you will make a journey across the circle.'* Watch the first child cross the circle by hopping. Say, *'Now change the way you make your journey.'* Encourage them to think of a way to change the journey (e.g. jump). Give a turn to each person in the circle. Encourage the use of the vocabulary, 'make the journey' and 'change how you make the journey'.

**relax and
have fun**

Session 18

Materials

- Cress seeds to check for growth.
- Top up water.
- Cube shape.
- Tambourine and shaker bells.
- Picture of nose (see appendix).
- Two small covered boxes containing two different scents (e.g. bath salts, orange peel).

Opening song

(Sitting)

Sit in a circle. Explain that you will be singing your song today. Practise singing together with actions:

> I can touch my ears (clap twice)
> I can touch my nose (clap twice)
> I can touch my eyes (clap twice)
> And I can touch my hands (spread out fingers and wiggle them) (clap twice)
> I use my ears to hear
> I use my nose to smell
> I use my eyes to see
> I use my mouth to taste
> I use my hands to feel
> **I use all my senses.**

Encourage the children to count on their fingers the five senses, saying, *'I hear, I smell, I see, I taste, I feel.'*

Growing things – What do we need?

(Standing)

Ask the children to talk in pairs to see if they remember what growing things need. Bring in the science rabbit and lay out the picture cards for light, water and nutrients/food when the children remember them. Encourage them if necessary. Check the cress seeds for progress. Ask if they are changing and comment as necessary. Encourage the words 'growing', 'changing' and 'longer'. Compare with the non-progress of the cube. Ask the children for their thoughts.

Different force, different sound

(Standing)

Explain that you will pass around a tambourine or shaker bells for the children to try.

When everyone has taken a turn, say, *'You can shake this gently and it makes a quiet sound* [demonstrate] *and you can use more force and shake it strongly and it makes a louder sound* [demonstrate]. *I will pass it around the circle. When I say "strong", the person who is holding it has to shake it strongly and when I say "gentle", the person holding it has to shake it gently.'*

All stand up and play this game.

Super senses – Smell

(Sitting)

Sit down and place the picture of a nose on the carpet in the middle of the circle.

Say, *'I can do something with my nose.'* Model sniffing something. Ask the children to think about what they can do with their noses. Tell them to talk to someone next to them about it.

After a minute or so bring the focus back to the circle and share their answers. If the children don't give an answer say, *'You had a good think.'* Finally ask, *'What can I do with my nose?'* Repeat the answer, *'Yes, I can smell with my nose. Let's use our sense of smell to find out things.'*

Lay out two small covered containers containing two different scents (e.g. bath salts and orange peel). Say, *'Let's use our sense of smell to find what is in the pots.'* Model smelling the pots and your reaction. Pass the first pot around the circle, commenting as each child smells it and reacts (e.g. *'Jasmine is smelling the pot to find out what is in it. She looks as if she likes the smell.'* Next, pass the second pot around and repeat the same procedure.

> **use pondering take your time**

Now ask, *'What can we use to find out what is in the pots? Talk to the person next to you'* (for half a minute). Focus back in the circle and listen to answers (you may find that the children say what is in the pot rather than how they can find out what is in the pot. Just focus them by repeating again, *'What can we use to find out if you are right?'*). Either combine the answers or develop them and say, *'We can use our noses to smell but we need to use our eyes to see as well.'* Uncover each pot and pass it around.

BE POSITIVE

63

Closing round – Changing journeys

(Standing)

Say to the children, *'Choose how you will make a journey across the circle.'* Watch the first child cross the circle by, for example, hopping. Say, *'Now change the way you make your journey.'*

Encourage them to think of a way to change the journey (e.g. jump). Give a turn to each person in the circle. Encourage the use of vocabulary – 'make the journey' and 'change how you make the journey'.

Session 19

```
Materials
• Cress seeds to check for growth.
• Top up water.
• Tambourine and wooden beater or triangle (different from last time).
• Cube shape.
• Another shaken instrument.
```

Sounds like this

(Sitting)

Say *'We are going to look at some musical instruments. They are things that make music.'* Lay out an instrument (e.g. a tambourine), and a different instrument from last time (e.g. a triangle or a wooden beater). In pairs, talk about how you would play these instruments. Pass the tambourine around for the children to share their ideas, then pass the second instrument around. Say that you are going to choose two children to play them as you all sing the opening song.

Opening song

(Sitting)

Sit in a circle. Explain that you will be singing your song today. Practise singing together with actions:

> I can touch my ears (clap twice)
> I can touch my nose (clap twice)
> I can touch my eyes (clap twice)
> And I can touch my hands (spread out fingers and wiggle them) (clap twice)
> I use my ears to hear
> I use my nose to smell
> I use my eyes to see
> I use my mouth to taste
> I use my hands to feel
> **I use all my senses.**

Encourage the children to count on their fingers the five senses, saying, *'I hear, I smell, I see, I taste, I feel.'*

Growing things – What do we need?

(Sitting and standing)

Ask the children to talk in pairs to see if they remember what growing things need. Bring in the science rabbit and the 'growing' picture. Encourage if necessary. Check the cress seeds for progress. Ask if they are changing and comment as necessary.

Encourage the words 'growing', 'changing' and 'longer'. Compare with the non-progress of the cube. Ask the children for their thoughts.

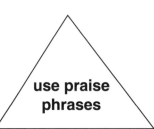

Chase the sound maker

(Standing)

One child stands in the middle with their eyes closed. Give a (shaken) instrument to one of the children and ask all the children to stand with their hands behind their backs. Tell the child in the middle that they will have to find out who is holding the sound maker. Ask them to open their eyes.

    The game is to ask a person in the circle, *'Have you got the sound maker?'* If they have, they must shake it behind their back. When the seeker is sure, then they say *'You have the sound maker.'* If they are wrong, they must keep guessing until they have chosen the right person. Take turns around the circle several times to encourage listening skills and the use of vocabulary.

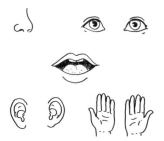

Review – What senses have I used?

Remind the children what the senses are and what we use them for. Ask the children in pairs to think about what senses they have used and listen to feedback. Emphasise – eyes to look and see, ears to hear the instruments, and hands to touch and feel. Ask what senses you haven't used.

Closing round – The listening song

(Standing)

To the tune of 'Here we go round the mulberry bush':

> I can use my listening ears, listening ears, listening ears,
> I can use my listening ears and I can hear a bee [All buzz].
>
> I can use my listening ears, listening ears, listening ears,
> I can use my listening ears and I can hear a cow [All moo].
>
> I can use my listening ears, listening ears, listening ears,
> I can use my listening ears and I can hear. [Stop] What can we hear?

Encourage the children to tell you what they can hear.

Session 20

```
┌─────────────────────────────────────────────────────────────────┐
                              Materials
   • Cress seeds to check for growth.
   • Top up water.
   • Magnetic shapes.
   • Tin tray.
   • Wooden board.
   • Large box.
   • Post-it notes and pen to record (optional).
   • Science rabbit.
   • 'Growing' picture cards.
   • See-through fish and opaque snake shapes.
   • Torch.
└─────────────────────────────────────────────────────────────────┘
```

Opening song

(Sitting)

Sit in a circle. Explain that you will be singing your song today. Practise singing together with actions:

> I can touch my ears (clap twice)
> I can touch my nose (clap twice)
> I can touch my eyes (clap twice)
> And I can touch my hands (spread out fingers and wiggle them) (clap twice)
> I use my ears to hear
> I use my nose to smell
> I use my eyes to see
> I use my mouth to taste
> I use my hands to feel
> **I use all my senses.**

Encourage the children to count on their fingers the five senses, saying, *'I hear, I smell, I see, I taste, I feel.'*

Amazing magnets

(Sitting)

Lay out the tin tray, the wooden board and a large book. Remind the children what happened last time when the magnets stuck to one surface even when it was upside-down.

Offer around the small magnetised shapes, asking the children to say which shape they will choose before they do so. Invite the children to put their shapes on to one of the surfaces. Then ponder with the group what will happen when you turn each surface upside-down. Ask the children to talk in pairs for a few moments about their ideas.

Choose three children to come and sit by a board. Take ideas from the group on the first board, then ask the child to turn it upside-down, and so on to the other two.

Recap that magnets stick to metal but not to wood or paper. Say that to remember it we could put a piece of sticky paper on each one with a tick if it sticks and an x if it does not.

use
pondering
take your
time

Growing things – What do we need?

(Standing)

Ask the children to talk in pairs to see if they remember what growing things need. Bring in the science rabbit and the 'growing' picture. Encourage if necessary. Check the cress seeds for progress. Ask if they are changing and comment as necessary. Encourage the words 'growing', 'changing' and 'longer'. Compare with the non-progress of the cube. Ask the children for their thoughts.

BE
POSITIVE

See-through fish and opaque snake

(Sitting)

Lay out a selection of clear fish shapes and opaque snake shapes. Say to the children, *'Here is the torch. Shine it on to the opaque snake or the see-through fish.'* Ensure that children use the words 'see-through' and 'opaque'. Give each person in the circle a turn. You can ask the children to choose the next person for their turn.

Closing round – Torch on and torch off

(Standing)

Tell the children that they will pretend to be torches. When you say, *'Switch your torches on'* they will open their eyes, and when you say *'Switch your torches off'* they will close their eyes.

Practice this as a group. Then say, *'I will point at someone and say, "Julia, switch on your torch" or "Julia, switch off your torch" and you have to do as I say.'*

relax and
have fun

Session 21

```
                        Materials
• Tambourine or shaker bells.
• Three items: a push-along toy, a pull-along toy with string attached and a
  large plastic or cardboard box.
• Cress seeds to check for growth.
• Top up water.
• Cube shapes.
• Pictures of growing/non-growing things.
```

Opening song

(Sitting)

Sit in a circle. Explain that you will be singing your song today. Practise singing together with actions:

> I can touch my ears (clap twice)
> I can touch my nose (clap twice)
> I can touch my eyes (clap twice)
> And I can touch my hands (spread out fingers and wiggle them) (clap twice)
> I use my ears to hear
> I use my nose to smell
> I use my eyes to see
> I use my mouth to taste
> I use my hands to feel
> **I use all my senses.**

Encourage the children to count on their fingers the five senses, saying, *'I hear, I smell, I see, I taste, I feel.'*

Different force, different sound

(Standing)

Explain that you will pass around a tambourine or shaker bells for the children to try.

When everyone has take a turn say, *'You can shake this gently and it makes a quiet sound* [demonstrate] *and you can use more force and shake it strongly and it makes a louder sound* [demonstrate]. *I will pass it around the circle. When I say "strong", the person who is holding it has to shake it strongly and when I say "gentle" the person holding it has to shake it gently.'* All stand up and play this game.

Push and pull (force)

(Sitting)

Lay out three items – a push-along toy, a pull-along toy with string attached, and a large plastic or cardboard box. Ask the children for their ideas on what the toys are and what you would do with them. Say, *'If you want to make a toy move you have to use force. That is what we call it when we push or pull something.'* Ask each person in the group which force they will use – push or pull – and then choose a toy to do this. Encourage use of the words 'push' and 'pull' (e.g. *'I will push the toy', 'I will pull the string'*). When everyone has taken a turn invite ideas as to what you could do to move the box.

use pondering take your time

Encourage use of the words 'forwards', 'backwards', 'towards' and 'sideways' as in 'Push the box forwards, pull the box backwards and towards John.'

Growing and not growing

(Sitting)

Place the cube and the cress seeds in the middle of the circle. Pass around a feely bag which contains pictures of growing things and man-made things. Children are invited to take one picture and place it next to either the cube or the cress seeds.

(We suggest that you make a collage of this and keep it next to the cube and the cress seeds in the window.)

Talk about the properties of the two categories. Remind the children of the words 'water', 'light' and 'nutrients'.

BE POSITIVE

Closing round – Changing journeys

(Standing)

Say to the children, *'Choose how you will make a journey across the circle.'* Watch the first child cross the circle by, for example, hopping. Say, *'Now change the way you make your journey.'* Encourage them to think of a way to change the journey (e.g. jump). Give a turn to each person in the circle. Encourage the use of vocabulary – 'make the journey' and 'change how you make the journey'.

Session 22

Materials

- Pictures of toys (e.g. scooter, bicycle, skateboard).
- Feely bag containing pictures of fur- and feather-covered creatures, and people.
- Torch.

Opening song

(Sitting)

Sit in a circle. Explain that you will be singing your song today. Practise singing together with actions:

> I can touch my *ears* (clap twice)
> I can touch my *nose* (clap twice)
> I can touch my *eyes* (clap twice)
> And I can touch my *hands* (spread out fingers and wiggle them) (clap twice)
> I use my ears to hear
> I use my nose to smell
> I use my eyes to see
> I use my mouth to taste
> I use my hands to feel
> **I use all my senses.**

Encourage the children to count on their fingers the five senses, saying, *'I hear, I smell, I see, I taste, I feel.'*

Happy song

(Standing)

Stand up and walk round in a circle singing:

> If you're happy and you know it clap your hands,
> If you're happy and you know it clap your hands,
> If you're happy and you know it and you really want to show it, if you're happy and you know it...

Stop and sing, *'Clap your hands.'*

Repeat with *'Give me a smile.'*

Forces we know – Push and pull

(Sitting)

Talk about the toys the children might use or see older children using (e.g. scooter, bike, skateboard, pram, pull-along toys and roller-skates). Talk about what force is used to make them move – push or pull. Show any pictures you may have.

> **use
> pondering
> take your
> time**

Fur, feathers and clothes

(Sitting, then standing)

Pass the feely bag around with pictures of fur- and feather-covered creatures, and people (see appendices). When everyone has taken a picture ask them to talk about being covered and keeping warm by fur, feathers or clothes. Stand up and ask the children to form into small groups according to what set of cards they have. Ask them to decide how else their group is different in the way that they move, and then ask each group to act out how they would move if they were in that picture.

Closing round – Torch on and torch off

(Standing)

Tell the children that they will pretend to be torches. When you say, *'Switch your torches on'* they will open their eyes, and when you say , *'Switch your torches off'* they will close their eyes.

Practise this as a group. Next, choose one person to be the battery while everyone stands with their eyes closed. The battery then goes round, touches each child's shoulder and says, *'Now you have power you can light up.'* That person then opens their eyes.

Session 23

Materials

- Tambourine.
- Triangle or wooden beater.
- Feely bag containing pictures of fur- and feather-covered creatures, and people.
- Two bar magnets.
- Safety hand mirror.

Sounds like this

(Sitting)

Say, *'We are going to look at some musical instruments. They are things that make music.'* Lay out an instrument (e.g. a tambourine), and a different instrument from last time (e.g. a triangle or a wooden beater). In pairs, talk about how you would play these instruments. Pass the tambourine around for the children to share their ideas, then pass the second instrument around. Say that you are going to choose two children to play instruments while you all sing the opening song.

Opening song

(Sitting)

Sit in a circle. Explain that you will be singing your song today. Practise singing together with actions:

I can touch my ears (clap twice)
I can touch my nose (clap twice)
I can touch my eyes (clap twice)
And I can touch my hands (spread out fingers and wiggle them) (clap twice)
I use my ears to hear
I use my nose to smell
I use my eyes to see
I use my mouth to taste
I use my hands to feel
I use all my senses.

Encourage the children to count on their fingers the five senses, saying, *'I hear, I smell, I see, I taste, I feel.'*

BE
POSITIVE

Fur, feathers and clothes

(Sitting, then standing)

Pass the feely bag around with pictures of fur- and feather-covered creatures, and people (see appendices). When everyone has taken a picture ask them to talk about being covered and keeping warm by fur, feathers or clothes. Stand up and ask the children to form into small groups according to what set of cards they have. Ask them to decide how else their group is different, for example, in the way that they move, then ask each group to act out how they would move if they were in that picture.

Magnetic forces

(Sitting)

Using two bar magnets show how one end will attract and one end will repel. Pass it around the circle for the children to try. Invite two children to stand in the middle of the circle with their arms held out to pretend to be two bars. When you say *'attract'* their hands go together and when you say *'repel'* they come apart again. Continue until all have had a turn.

> **use
> pondering
> take your
> time**

Closing round – Pass a smile in the mirror

(Standing in a circle)

Song (which will be built up over the coming session).
   Make your hand into a pretend mirror:

I look in the mirror and what do I see? I see my face looking back at me.

Session 24

Materials

- Tambourine or shaker bells.
- Two red and two white squares of any material for each group of children.
- Feely bag containing pictures of fur- and feather-covered creatures, and people.

Opening song

(Sitting)

Sit in a circle. Explain that you will be singing your song today. Practise singing together with actions:

> I can touch my ears (clap twice)
> I can touch my nose (clap twice)
> I can touch my eyes (clap twice)
> And I can touch my hands (spread out fingers and wiggle them) (clap twice)
> I use my ears to hear
> I use my nose to smell
> I use my eyes to see
> I use my mouth to taste
> I use my hands to feel
> **I use all my senses.**

Encourage the children to count on their fingers the five senses, saying, *'I hear, I smell, I see, I taste, I feel.'*

Different force, different sound

(Standing)

Explain that you will pass around a tambourine or shaker bells for the children to try. When everyone has take a turn say, *'You can shake this gently and it makes a quiet sound* [demonstrate] *and you can use more force and shake it strongly and it makes a louder sound* [demonstrate]. *I will pass it around the circle. When I say "strong", the person who is holding it has to shake it strongly and when I say "gentle" the person holding it has to shake it gently.'*

Changing patterns

(Sitting)

Show the children four squares, two white and two red. Say that you can make patterns with them. Divide the group into two. Give each group four of these squares and ask them to make a pattern. Come back into the circle, look at the patterns and compare them for similarities and differences.

> use
> pondering
> take your
> time

Change – ask the children to work out with you what they would need to change to make the patterns look the same.

Fur, feathers and clothes

(Sitting, then standing)

Pass around the feely bag containing pictures of fur- and feather-covered creatures, and people (see appendices). When everyone has taken a picture, ask them to talk about being covered and keeping warm by fur, feathers or clothes. Stand up and ask the children to form into small groups according to what set of cards they have. Ask them to decide how else their group is different, for example, in the way that they move, then ask each group to act out how they would move if they were in that picture. Ask the children to think about how they would use their voices. Talk about the differences between animals, birds and humans.

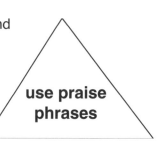

use praise phrases

Closing round – Pass the smile song

(Standing)

Ask the children to hold up their hands as if they were looking into a mirror. Then sing:

I look in the mirror and what do I see? I see a friendly face looking back at me. And I'm smiling, smiling. A smile makes me feel good inside. So I'm smiling, smiling and feeling good inside.

Session 25

Materials

- Two bar magnets.
- Two jars containing water; salt and instant coffee.
- Stirrer.

Opening Song

(Sitting)

Sit in a circle. Explain that you will be singing your song today. Practise singing together with actions:

> I can touch my ears (clap twice)
> I can touch my nose (clap twice)
> I can touch my eyes (clap twice)
> And I can touch my hands (spread out fingers and wiggle them) (clap twice)
> I use my ears to hear
> I use my nose to smell
> I use my eyes to see
> I use my mouth to taste
> I use my hands to feel
> **I use all my senses.**

Encourage the children to count on their fingers the five senses, saying, *'I hear, I smell, I see, I taste, I feel.'*

Review – What senses have I used?

Remind the children what the senses are and what we use them for. Ask the children in pairs to think about what senses they have used and listen to feedback. Emphasise – eyes to look and see, ears to hear the instruments, hands to touch and feel. Ask what senses you haven't used.

**use
pondering
take your
time**

Magnetic forces

(Sitting)

Using two bar magnets, show the children that one end will attract and one end will repel. Pass it around the circle for the children to try. Invite two children to stand in the middle of the circle with their arms out to pretend to be two bars. When you say *'attract'* their hands go together, and when you say *'repel'* they come apart again. Continue until all have had a turn.

Happy song

(Standing)

Stand up and walk round in a circle, singing:

> If you're happy and you know it clap your hands,
> If you're happy and you know it clap your hands,
> If you're happy and you know it and you really want to
> show it, if you're happy and you know it . . .

Stop and sing, *'Clap your hands.'*

Repeat with *'Give me a smile.'*

Dissolving and changing

(Sitting)

Lay out two small jars of water. Pass around a tub of salt for the children to inspect. Talk in pairs about what will happen if you put the salt into water. Listen to ideas. Invite a child to tip some salt into the water, stir it and pass it around the circle for the children to inspect. Use the vocabulary 'disappear' and 'dissolve'.

    Pass around a jar of coffee for the children to inspect. Talk in pairs about what will happen if you put the coffee into water. Listen to ideas. Invite a child to tip some coffee into the water, stir it and pass it around the circle for the children to inspect. Point out that you cannot see through the jar of coffee as it is opaque.

Closing round – Journeys

(Standing)

Say, *'You will be making a journey across the circle. I will make my journey by jumping.'*

    Demonstrate this. Encourage children to use the word 'journey' and to think of different ways of making the journey across the circle (e.g. hopping, rolling, slithering, walking).

Session 26

Materials

- Cardboard box (e.g. shoe box).
- Torch.
- Small cloth for a blanket.
- Pictures of night-time (see appendices).
- Two jars each of water; icing sugar and bicarbonate of soda.
- Stirrer.

Opening song

(Sitting)

Sit in a circle. Explain that you will be singing your song today. Practise singing together with actions:

> I can touch my ears (clap twice)
> I can touch my nose (clap twice)
> I can touch my eyes (clap twice)
> And I can touch my hands (spread out fingers and wiggle them) (clap twice)
> I use my ears to hear
> I use my nose to smell
> I use my eyes to see
> I use my mouth to taste
> I use my hands to feel
> **I use all my senses.**

Encourage the children to count on their fingers the five senses, saying, *'I hear, I smell, I see, I taste, I feel.'*

Day and night

(Sitting)

'Last time we looked into the box we couldn't see very much.' Ponder why. *'It was dark. The light couldn't get into the box. What did we do? We used a torch to give us light. When we turned it off it was dark in the box.'*

Ponder that dark happens when there is no light. *'The box was dark for a little while. When is it dark for a long time? When we go to sleep. Night-time. It is dark at night. What do we do?*

'Let's hear a night-time story.' Lay out a small cloth for a blanket in the middle of the circle. *'Little rabbit went to sleep. He thought everyone was asleep. But they weren't. Out of a corner crept Mr Fox. Mr Fox didn't go to sleep until very late. He crept around in the dark looking for food.'*

> **use**
> **pondering**
> **take your**
> **time**

Make up a story using Mr Fox and invite the children to say what will happen next.

Bring in the concepts of dark and night-time, not much light to see by, sharp-eyed animals seeing in the dark. Encourage the children to talk about people they know who go to work at night.

At the end, hold up a sun shape and say the sun came up slowly and all the night creatures went home to bed, and people and daytime creatures started to wake up.

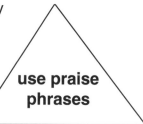

use praise phrases

Happy song

(Standing)

Stand up and walk round in a circle singing:

> If you're happy and you know it clap your hands,
> If you're happy and you know it clap your hands,
> If you're happy and you know it and you really want to show it, if you're happy and you know it...

Stop and sing, *'Clap your hands.'*

Repeat with *'Give me a smile.'*

Dissolving and changing

(Sitting)

Lay out two small jars of clear water. Pass around a tub of icing sugar for the children to inspect. Talk in pairs about what will happen if you put the icing sugar into water. Listen to ideas. Invite a child to tip the icing sugar into the water, stir it and pass it around the circle for the children to inspect. Use the vocabulary 'disappear' and 'dissolve'.

Pass around a tub of bicarbonate of soda for the children to inspect. Talk in pairs about what will happen if you put it into water. Take ideas. Invite a child to tip it into the water, stir it around and pass it round the circle for the children to inspect the fizzy liquid.

Closing round – Journeys in the light

(Standing)

Say, *'You will be making a journey across the circle. You will pretend it is daytime and you can see very well because there is a lot of light. I will make my journey by jumping.'*

Ask the children where the light is coming from. Ask them to cross the circle by creeping, then walking, then tiptoeing.

Session 27

Materials

- A push-along toy, a pull-along toy with string attached, and six cube shapes.
- Two jars containing white vinegar, and salt and bicarbonate of soda.
- Stirrer.
- Coloured marbles in a jar (two colours only).

Opening song

(Sitting)

Sit in a circle. Explain that you will be singing your song today. Practise singing together with actions:

> I can touch my *ears* (clap twice)
> I can touch my *nose* (clap twice)
> I can touch my *eyes* (clap twice)
> And I can touch my *hands* (spread out fingers and wiggle them) (clap twice)
> I use my *ears* to hear
> I use my *nose* to smell
> I use my *eyes* to see
> I use my *mouth* to taste
> I use my *hands* to feel
> **I use all my senses.**

Encourage the children to count on their fingers the five senses, saying, *'I hear, I smell, I see, I taste, I feel.'*

Force – push and lift

(Sitting)

Lay out a push-along toy, a pull-along toy with string attached, and six cubes. Ask the children for their ideas on what the toys are and what you would do with them. Remind them that *'if you want to make a toy move you have to use "a force". That is what we call it when we push or pull something.'* Then talk about a different force used to lift things. Ask one of the children to place the cubes on top of each other to make a tower. Model moving it by pushing gently, pulling gently or lifting gently. Set the challenge for the children to use a force to move the tower of bricks without dropping any.

Review and encourage the children to use the phrases 'I pushed two bricks', 'I pulled the bricks', 'I lifted the bricks'. Use the words 'gently' and 'strongly'.

81

Dissolving and changing

(Sitting)

Do give adequate safety warning before handing the vinegar around and before adding the bicarbonate of soda. Ensure that the children keep their faces away from the liquids.

Lay out two small jars of white vinegar. Pass around a tub of salt for the children to inspect. Talk in pairs about what will happen if you put the salt into the vinegar. Listen to ideas. Invite a child to tip the salt into the vinegar, stir it and pass it around the circle for the children to inspect. Use the vocabulary 'disappear' and 'dissolve'.

Pass around a tub of bicarbonate of soda for the children to inspect. Talk in pairs about what will happen if you put it into vinegar. Listen to ideas. Invite a child to tip some soda into vinegar, stir it and pass it around the circle for the children to inspect the fizzy liquid.

> **use
> pondering
> take your
> time**

Coloured marbles

(Sitting)

The science rabbit says, *'I have brought my jar of marbles. Can you help me to find out what colours I have got please?'* Pass around the jar several times. Each time a child takes out a marble, ask them to say what colour it is, and pass on the jar. Continue until all the marbles have gone.

Lay out the marbles in two lines and talk about being able to see that there are more of one colour when you lay them out like that.

Closing round – The listening song

(Standing)

To the tune of 'Here we go round the mulberry bush'.

> I can use my listening ears, listening ears, listening ears,
> I can use my listening ears and I can hear a bee [All buzz].
>
> I can use my listening ears, listening ears, listening ears,
> I can use my listening ears and I can hear a cow [All moo].
>
> I can use my listening ears, listening ears, listening ears,
> I can use my listening ears and I can
> hear...[Stop] What can we hear?

Encourage the children to tell you what they can hear.

> **relax and
> have fun**

Session 28

Materials

- Animal puppet.
- Pictures from sheets in appendices of hot and cold food.
- Pictures (or models) of fridge and cooker.
- Pencil.
- Two ring magnets.
- Three objects (one made of wood, one of metal and one of plastic).

Opening song

(Sitting)

Sit in a circle. Explain that you will be singing your song today. Practise singing together with actions:

> I can touch my ears (clap twice)
> I can touch my nose (clap twice)
> I can touch my eyes (clap twice)
> And I can touch my hands (spread out fingers and wiggle them) (clap twice)
> I use my ears to hear
> I use my nose to smell
> I use my eyes to see
> I use my mouth to taste
> I use my hands to feel
> **I use all my senses.**

Encourage the children to count on their fingers the five senses, saying, *'I hear, I smell, I see, I taste, I feel.'*

Keeping warm (food and drink)

(Sitting)

The science rabbit reminds the children that last time they looked at how clothes kept them warm. Encourage the children to use the words 'clothes keep us warm' and ask them to remember the clothes they looked at during the last session. This time they will be looking at food we eat when we are hot and food we eat when we are cold.

Lay out pictures of hot and cold food and drink. Ask the children to talk in pairs to try to remember which foods were hot (warming foods) and which were cold (cooling foods).

Lay out on one side of the circle the picture of a fridge and on the other side the picture of a cooker. Ask the children to place the food and drink in the correct place (by the cooker or by the fridge). When all the pictures have been placed ponder what the cooker does to make the food or drink hot. Take ideas on other food and drink they can think of which is hot or cold.

```
use
pondering
take your
time
```

Force – Magnets

(Sitting)

Hold a pencil. Drop a ring magnet over the top of it. Invite a child to drop another ring magnet over it and see what happens. Experiment with different sides of the magnet so that they either attract or repel. Then put the second magnet on the pencil so that it repels and hovers just over the other magnet. Invite children one by one to push the top magnet down to see what happens. Ask them to push it gently or use a lot of force.

BE POSITIVE

Closing round – Wood, metal and plastic

(Standing)

Pass around three objects, one made of wood, one of metal and one of plastic. Lay them out in a circle and invite the children to name them and stand on one of the surfaces.

Session 29

Materials

- Two bar magnets.
- Animal puppet.
- Large feely bag containing jacket, sock, glove, hat and scarf.
- Tambourine or shaker bells.

Opening song

(Sitting)

Sit in a circle. Explain that you will be singing your song today. Practise singing together with actions:

> I can touch my ears (clap twice)
> I can touch my nose (clap twice)
> I can touch my eyes (clap twice)
> And I can touch my hands (spread out fingers and wiggle them) (clap twice)
> I use my ears to hear
> I use my nose to smell
> I use my eyes to see
> I use my mouth to taste
> I use my hands to feel
> **I use all my senses.**

Encourage the children to count on their fingers the five senses, saying, *'I hear, I smell, I see, I taste, I feel.'*

Magnetic forces

(Sitting)

Using two bar magnets show that one end will attract and one end repel. Pass it around the circle for the children to try. Invite two children to stand in the middle of the circle with their arms held out to pretend to be two bars. When you say *'attract'* their hands go together, and when you say *'repel'* they come apart. Continue until all have had a turn.

Keep me warm (clothes)

(Sitting)

The science rabbit says that he doesn't get very cold because he is wearing something warm. The children have to guess what it is. The little animal says, *'Yes, I've got fur to keep me warm.'* He then asks the children to talk in pairs about what they wear to keep warm.

Take out of a large feely bag the following items, asking each time, *'Would we wear this to keep warm?'*:

jacket   sock   glove   hat   scarf

Talk about why you would wear these things.

Different force, different sound

(Standing)

Explain that you will pass around a tambourine or shaker bells for the children to try.

When everyone has taken a turn, say, *'You can shake this gently and it makes a quiet sound* [demonstrate] *and you can use more force and shake it strongly and it makes a louder sound* [demonstrate]. *I will pass it around the circle. When I say "strong", the person who is holding it has to shake it strongly and when I say "gentle" the person holding it has to shake it gently.'*

All stand up and play this game. Put the instrument away. Say that you can make loud or soft noises using parts of your body. Experiment with soft claps and loud claps, hands together, hands on knees and foot stamps on the floor.

Closing round – Musical bodies

(Standing)

Talk about making musical sounds with parts of our bodies.

Demonstrate:

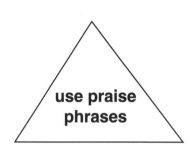

- Clap hands
- Pat knees
- Pat blown-out cheeks
- Pat hollowed cheeks
- Tap feet, use more force, then stamp feet.

Get the children to try each sound in turn.

Experiment using different body parts and different force, and listen to the sounds.

Encourage use of words – 'forceful', 'less forceful', 'tap', 'clap', 'listen', 'sound', 'loud', 'quiet'.

Session 30

Materials

- Tumbler, plastic box, book and a cardboard box.
- Feely bag containing a selection of transparent and opaque materials/objects.
- Torch.
- Jar containing coloured marbles (two colours only).

Opening song

(Sitting)

Sit in a circle. Explain that you will be singing your song today. Practise singing together with actions:

> I can touch my ears (clap twice)
> I can touch my nose (clap twice)
> I can touch my eyes (clap twice)
> And I can touch my hands (spread out fingers and wiggle them) (clap twice)
> I use my ears to hear
> I use my nose to smell
> I use my eyes to see
> I use my mouth to taste
> I use my hands to feel
> **I use all my senses**.

Encourage the children to count on their fingers the five senses, saying, *'I hear, I smell, I see, I taste, I feel.'*

Will it let the light through?

(Sitting in a circle)

In the middle of a circle lay out the four objects you used before (e.g. a tumbler, a plastic box, a book, a cardboard box). Refresh the children's memory of the meaning of the words 'transparent', 'not see-through' and 'opaque'.

Pass around a feely bag. Each child takes out an object and says whether it is see-through/transparent or not see-through/opaque. Pass the torch around the circle for each child to test their ideas. Encourage the use of vocabulary in this game.

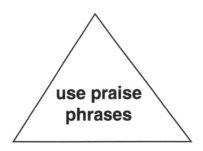

Coloured marbles

The science rabbit says, *'I have brought my jar of marbles. Can you help me to find out what colours I have got please?'* Pass around the jar several times. Each time, a person takes a marble, says what colour it is and passes on the jar. Continue until all the marbles have gone.

Lay out the marbles in two lines and talk about being able to see that there are more of one colour when you lay them out like that.

Musical bodies

(Standing)

Talk about making musical sounds using parts of our bodies.

Demonstrate:

- Clap hands
- Pat knees
- Pat blown-out cheeks
- Pat hollowed cheeks
- Tap feet, use more force, then stamp feet.

relax and have fun

Get children to try each sound in turn.
Experiment using different body parts and different force, and listen to the sounds.
Encourage use of words – 'forceful', 'less forceful', 'tap', 'clap', 'listen', 'sound', 'loud', 'quiet'.

Closing round – Torch on and torch off

(Standing)

Tell the children to pretend to be torches. When you say, *'Switch your torches on'* they will open their eyes, and when you say, *'Switch your torches off'* they will close their eyes.
Practise this as a group. Next, choose one person to be the battery while everyone stands with their eyes closed. The battery then goes around, touches each child's shoulder and says, *'Now you have power you can light up.'* That person then opens their eyes.

Session 31

> ## Materials
> - Feely bag containing pictures of fur- and feather-covered creatures, and people.
> - Feely bag containing inanimate objects (e.g. plastic brick, glove, spoon).
> - Pencil.
> - Two ring magnets.

Opening song

(Sitting)

Sit in a circle. Explain that you will be singing your song today. Practise singing together with actions:

> I can touch my ears (clap twice)
> I can touch my nose (clap twice)
> I can touch my eyes (clap twice)
> And I can touch my hands (spread out fingers and wiggle them) (clap twice)
> I use my ears to hear
> I use my nose to smell
> I use my eyes to see
> I use my mouth to taste
> I use my hands to feel
> **I use all my senses**.

Encourage the children to count on their fingers the five senses, saying, *'I hear, I smell, I see, I taste, I feel.'*

Fur, feathers and clothes

(Sitting, then standing)

Pass around the feely bag containing pictures of fur- and feather-covered creatures, and people. Talk with the group how all these things are alive. Stand up and ask the children to form into small groups according to what pictures they have. Ask them to decide how else their group is different in the way they do things (e.g. walk, run, sit). Ask the groups to act out how they would perform each movement if they were the animal in that picture. Ask the groups to think about how they would use their voices. Talk about the differences between animals, birds and humans.

From a different feely bag take out some inanimate objects such as a brick, a glove and a spoon. Ask if these things are alive. Talk about them being made in a factory or workshop.

> **use**
> **pondering**
> **take your**
> **time**

Force – Magnets

(Sitting)

Hold a pencil. Drop a ring magnet over the top of it. Invite a child to drop another ring magnet over it and see what happens. Experiment with different sides of the magnet so that they either attract or repel. Then put the second magnet on the pencil so that it repels and hovers just over the other magnet. Invite the children one by one to push the top magnet down to see what happens. Ask them to push it gently or use a lot of force.

Closing round – Journeys

(Standing)

Say, *'You will be making a journey across the circle. I will make my journey by jumping.'*

Demonstrate this. Encourage the children to use the word 'journey' and to think of different ways of making that journey across the circle (e.g. hopping, rolling, slithering, walking).

Session 32

> **Materials**
> - Feely bag containing pictures of sense organs (nose, mouth, eyes, ears).
> - Tambourine or shaker bells.

Opening song

(Sitting)

Sit in a circle. Explain that you will be singing your song today. Practise singing together with actions:

> I can touch my ears (clap twice)
> I can touch my nose (clap twice)
> I can touch my eyes (clap twice)
> And I can touch my hands (spread out fingers and wiggle them) (clap twice)
> I use my ears to hear
> I use my nose to smell
> I use my eyes to see
> I use my mouth to taste
> I use my hands to feel
> **I use all my senses.**

Encourage the children to count on their fingers the five senses, saying, *'I hear, I smell, I see, I taste, I feel.'*

Using our senses

(Sitting, then standing)

Pass around a feely bag containing various pictures of the sense organs. Invite each children in the group to take one, then say, *'Eyes stand up, ears stand up, nose stand up, mouth stand up, hands stand up.'*

Say, *'We are going to play a game where I say what I need to do, for example, hear, and people who have a picture of something you hear with can cross to a new place in the circle'* [change places]. Then say:

> Change places if you help me to see.
> Change places if you help me to hear.
> Change places if you help me to touch.
> Change places if you help me to smell.
> Change places if you help me to taste.

Then say, *'When I say "all the senses" everyone can change places.'*
Hold on to the pictures for the closing round.

Different force, different sound

(Standing)

Explain that you will pass around a tambourine or shaker bells for the children to try. When everyone has taken a turn say, *'You can shake this gently and it makes a quiet sound* [demonstrate] *and you can use more force and shake it strongly and it makes a louder sound* [demonstrate]. *I will pass it around the circle. When I say "strong", the person who is holding it has to shake it strongly and when I say "gentle" the person holding it has to shake it gently.'*

    All stand up and play this game. Put the instrument away. Say that you can make loud or soft noises with your body. Experiment with soft claps and loud claps, hands together, hands on knees and foot stamps on the floor. Talk about using more or less force.

> **use
> pondering
> take your
> time**

Closing round – 'I can help you'

(Sitting)

Pass around the feely bag. Say, *'I am going to go around the circle and ask you to tell me what picture you are holding and what that part of your body helps you to do.'*

    Encourage the children by modelling this for them:

'I have got an ear, it helps me to hear.'
'I have got hands, they help me to feel.'

92

Session 33

> ## Materials
> - Feely bag containing inanimate objects (e.g. glove, spoon, ball). Include two or three pictures of animals.
> - Three coloured plastic tinted sheets, one red, one yellow and one blue.
> - Three objects (one made of wood, one of metal and one of plastic).

Opening song

(Sitting)

Sit in a circle. Explain that you will be singing your song today. Practise singing together with actions:

> I can touch my ears (clap twice)
> I can touch my nose (clap twice)
> I can touch my eyes (clap twice)
> And I can touch my hands (spread out fingers and wiggle them) (clap twice)
> I use my ears to hear
> I use my nose to smell
> I use my eyes to see
> I use my mouth to taste
> I use my hands to feel
> **I use all my senses.**

Encourage the children to count on their fingers the five senses, saying, *'I hear, I smell, I see, I taste, I feel.'*

Alive and not alive (manufactured)

(Sitting)

Pass around a feely bag containing a selection of inanimate objects (e.g. glove, spoon, ball). Include two or three pictures of animals. The children have to decide which objects are alive and which are manufactured. Form into two groups according to their objects or pictures.

Musical bodies

(Standing)

Talk about making musical sounds with parts of our bodies. Demonstrate:

- Clap hands
- Pat knees
- Pat blown-out cheeks

- Pat hollowed cheeks
- Tap feet, use more force, then stamp feet.

Get the children to do each sound in turn. Experiment using different body parts and different force, and listen to the sounds.

Encourage use of words – 'forceful', 'less forceful', 'tap', 'clap', 'listen', 'sound', 'loud', 'quiet'

> relax and
> have fun

Changing colours

(Sitting)

Take three coloured plastic tinted sheets – one red, one yellow and one blue. Ask the children to name the colours.

Ask, *'What will happen if we put one colour on top of another colour?'* Ponder. *'We could get a different colour.'* Invite the children to put one sheet on top of the other. Ask them to say what colour they see. Try two sheets together and then all three sheets. Talk about this with the children.

> **use
> pondering
> take your
> time**

Closing game – Wood, metal and plastic

(Standing)

Pass round three objects, one made of wood, one of metal and one of plastic. Lay them out in a circle and invite the children to name and point to one of the surfaces.

Session 34

Materials
- A push-along toy, a pull-along toy with string attached, and six cubes.
- Three coloured plastic tinted sheets, one red, one yellow and one blue.
- Pencil.
- Two ring magnets.

Opening song

(Sitting)

Sit in a circle. Explain that you will be singing your song today. Practise singing together with actions:

> I can touch my ears (clap twice)
> I can touch my nose (clap twice)
> I can touch my eyes (clap twice)
> And I can touch my hands (spread out fingers and wiggle them) (clap twice)
> I use my ears to hear
> I use my nose to smell
> I use my eyes to see
> I use my mouth to taste
> I use my hands to feel
> **I use all my senses.**

Encourage the children to count on their fingers the five senses, saying, *'I hear, I smell, I see, I taste, I feel.'*

Force – Push and lift

(Sitting)

Lay out a push-along toy, a pull-along toy with string attached, and six cubes. Ask the children for their ideas on what the toys are and what you would do with them. Remind them that *'If you want to make a toy move you have to use "a force". That is what we call it when we push or pull something.'* Then talk about a different force used to lift things. Ask one of the children to place the cubes on top of each other to make a tower. Model moving it by pushing gently, pulling gently or lifting gently. Set a challenge for the children to use a force to move the tower of bricks without dropping any.

Review and encourage the children to use the words, 'I pushed the bricks', 'I pulled the bricks', 'I lifted the bricks'.

Changing colours

(Sitting)

Take three coloured plastic tinted sheets – one red, one yellow and one blue. Ask the children to name the colours.

Ask, *'What will happen if we put one sheet on top of another sheet?'* Ponder. *'We will get a different colour.'* Experiment with putting one sheet on top of the other. Ask the children to name the colour produced. Try using two different combinations and then all three sheets. Talk about this with the children.

> **use**
> **pondering**
> **take your**
> **time**

Force – Magnets

(Sitting)

Hold a pencil. Drop a ring magnet over the top of it. Invite a child to drop another ring magnet over it and see what happens. Experiment with different sides of the magnet so that they either attract or repel. Then put the second magnet on the pencil so that it repels and hovers just over the other magnet. Invite the children one by one to push the top magnet down to see what happens. Ask them to push it gently or use a lot of force.

Closing round – The listening song

(Standing)

To the tune of 'Here we go round the mulberry bush':

> I can use my listening ears, listening ears, listening ears,
> I can use my listening ears and I can hear a bee [All buzz].
>
> I can use my listening ears, listening ears, listening ears,
> I can use my listening ears and I can hear a cow [All moo].
>
> I can use my listening ears, listening ears, listening ears,
> I can use my listening ears and I can hear ... [Stop] What can we hear?

Encourage the children to tell you what they can hear.

BE
POSITIVE

96

Session 35

> **Materials**
> - Cardboard box.
> - Torch.
> - Small cloth for a blanket.
> - Pictures of night-time (see appendices).
> - Sun shape.
> - Pencil.
> - Ring magnets.

Opening Song

(Sitting)

Sit in a circle. Explain that you will be singing your song today. Practise singing together with actions:

> I can touch my ears (clap twice)
> I can touch my nose (clap twice)
> I can touch my eyes (clap twice)
> And I can touch my hands (spread out fingers and wiggle them) (clap twice)
> I use my ears to hear
> I use my nose to smell
> I use my eyes to see
> I use my mouth to taste
> I use my hands to feel
> **I use all my senses.**

Encourage the children to count on their fingers the five senses, saying, *'I hear, I smell, I see, I taste, I feel.'*

Day and night

(Sitting)

'Last time we looked into the box we couldn't see very much.' Ponder why. *'It was dark. The light couldn't get into the box. What did we do? We used a torch to give us light. When we turned it off it was dark in the box.'*

Ponder that dark happens when there is no light. *'The box was dark for a little while. When is it dark for a long time? When we go to sleep. Night-time. It is dark at night. What do we do? Let's hear a night-time story.'*

Lay out a small cloth for a blanket in the middle of the circle. *'Little rabbit went to sleep. He thought everyone was asleep. But they weren't. Out of a corner crept Mr Fox. Mr Fox didn't go to sleep until very late. He crept around in the dark looking for food.'*

| use |
| pondering |
| take your |
| time |

97

Make up a story using Mr Fox and invite the children to say what might happen. Remind the children about the concepts of dark and night-time, not much light to see by, sharp-eyed animals seeing in the dark.

Encourage the children to talk about people they know who go to work at night.

At the end hold up a sun shape and say the sun came up slowly and all the night creatures went home to bed, and people and daytime creatures started to wake up.

Force – Magnets

(Sitting)

Hold a pencil. Drop a ring magnet over the top of it. Invite a child to drop another ring magnet over it and see what happens. Experiment with different sides of the magnet so that they either attract or repel. Then put the second magnet on the pencil so that it repels and hovers just over the other magnet. Invite children one by one to push the top magnet down to see what happens. Ask them to push it gently or use a lot of force.

use praise phrases

Closing round – Journeys in the light

(Standing)

Say, *'You will be making a journey across the circle. You will pretend it is daytime and you can see very well because there is a lot of light. I will make my journey by jumping.'*

Ask the children where the light is coming from. Ask them to cross the circle by creeping, then walking, then tiptoeing.

Session 36

Materials
- Three objects, one made of wood, one of metal and one of plastic.
- Animal puppet.
- Jar containing coloured marbles.

Opening Song

(Sitting)

Sit in a circle. Explain that you will be singing a song today. Practise singing together with actions:

I can touch my *ears* (clap twice)
I can touch my *nose* (clap twice)
I can touch my *eyes* (clap twice)
And I can touch my *hands* (spread out fingers and wiggle them) (clap twice).

Coloured marbles

The science rabbit says '*I have brought my jar of marbles. Can you help me to find out what colours I have got please?*'

Pass around the jar several times. Each time a child takes a marble, say what colour it is and pass on the jar. Continue until all the marbles have gone.

Lay out the marbles in two lines and talk about being able to see that there are more of one colour when you lay them out like that.

Musical bodies

(Standing)

Talk about making musical sounds with our bodies. Demonstrate:

- Clap hands
- Pat knees
- Pat blown-out cheeks
- Pat hollowed cheeks
- Tap feet, use more force, then stamp feet.

Ask the children to make each sound in turn.

Experiment using different body parts and different force, and listen to the sounds.

Encourage the use of words – 'forceful', 'less forceful', 'tap', 'clap', 'listen', 'sound', 'loud', 'quiet'.

Review – What senses have I used?

Remind the children what the senses are and what we use them for. Ask them in pairs to think about what senses they have used and listen to feedback. Emphasise – eyes to look and see, ears to hear the instruments, and hands to touch and feel. Ask what senses you haven't used.

> **use
> pondering
> take your
> time**

Closing round – Wood, metal and plastic

(Standing)

Pass round three objects, one made of wood, one of metal and one of plastic. Lay them out in a circle and invite the children to name and point to one of the surfaces.

Appendix: photocopiables

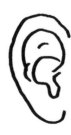

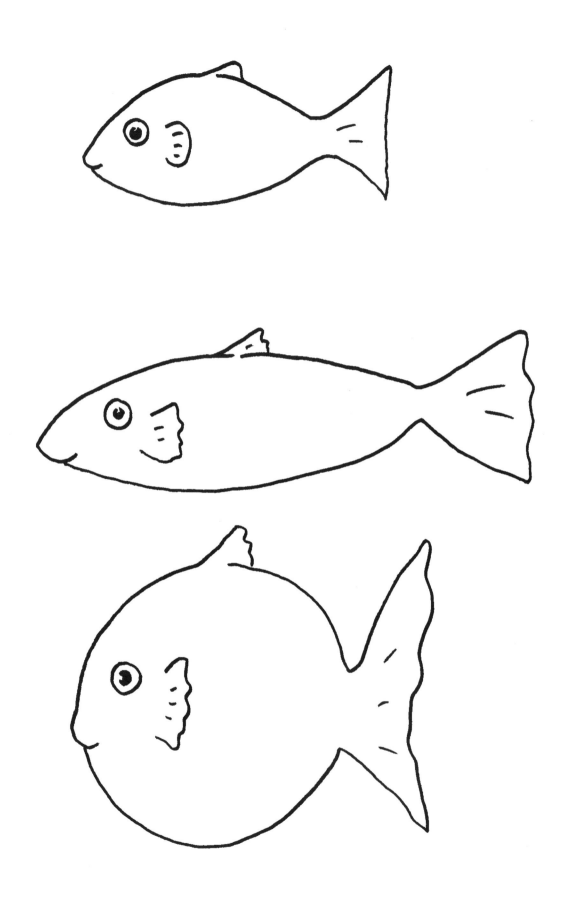

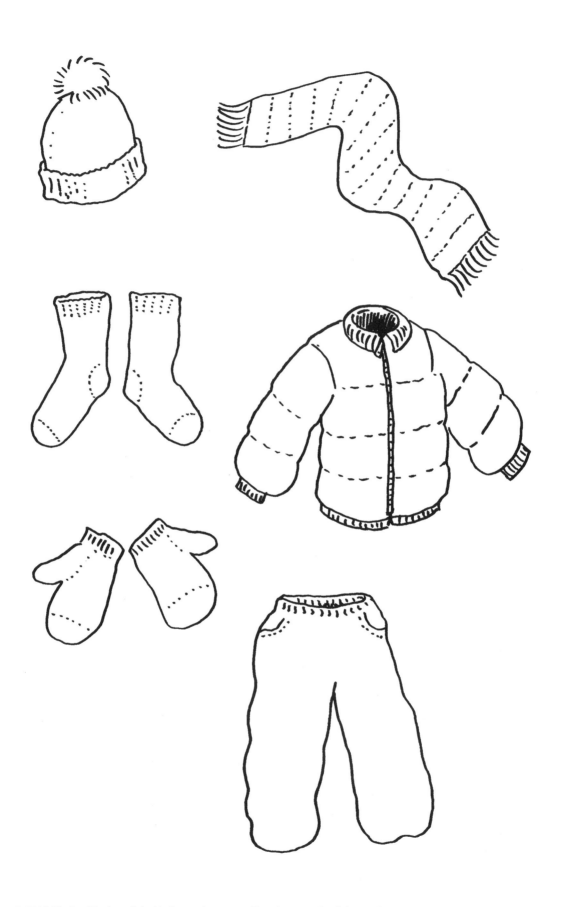

108

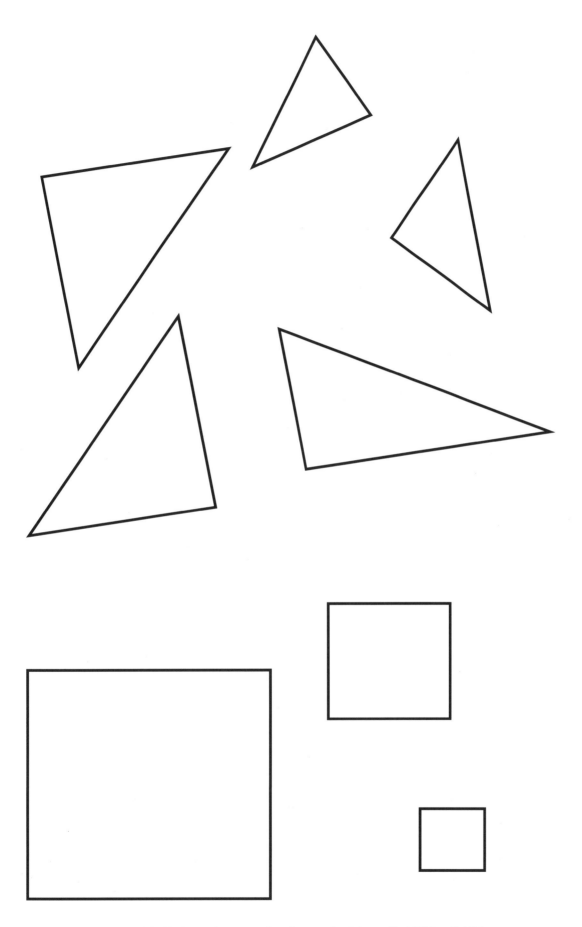

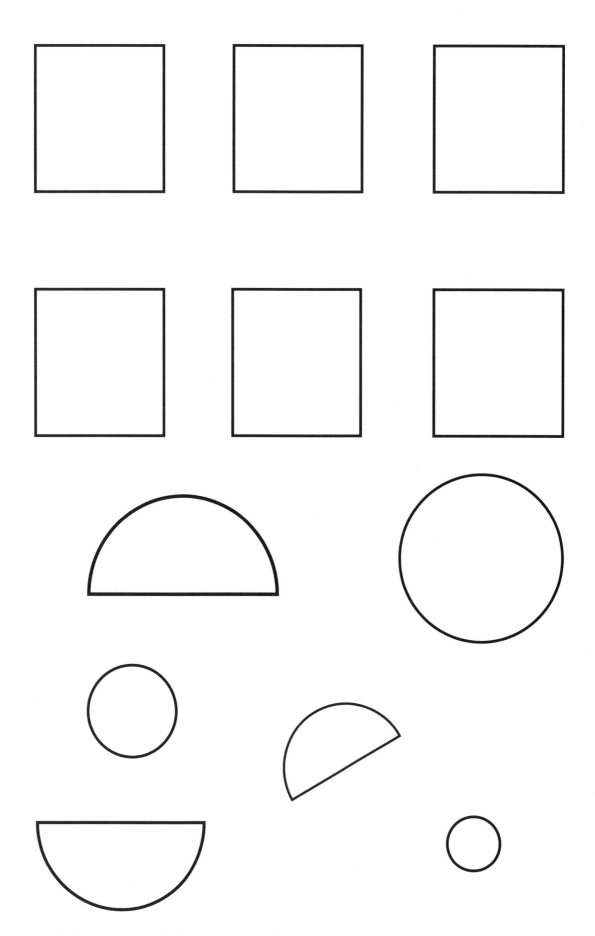

Help your children develop their language skills today!

Spirals This innovative new series addresses young children's language development needs in English, Maths and Science. Based on the spirals programme, developed by Marion Nash and successfully trialled in Plymouth schools, the books link work done in nursery or school with simple play-based activities for the children to do at home.

Ideal for Pre-school, KS1 & KS2

Focusing on English, Maths and Science the series consists of:

A class book that:

- employs a kinaesthetic approach, involving movement, singing, speaking and listening

- contains pre-planned sessions that can run over 2 terms or more

- has an accompanying Video CD providing explanations and demonstrations of the programme and its implementation, with comments from staff who have used it. Ideal for staff training!

An accompanying 'Activities for Home' book which includes:

- simple play-based activities focused on 'learning by doing' that you can photocopy and send home for parents to do with their children and reinforce the school-based sessions. The activities use everyday objects that are found at home and the book includes illustrated prompts to help parents.

> **No other books for language development focus on other core areas of the curriculum. Order yours today!**

Send your order to: David Fulton Publishers, The Chiswick Centre, 414 Chiswick High Road, London W4 5TF
Tel: 0208 996 3610 **Fax:** 0208 996 3622 **Email:** mail@fultonpublishers.co.uk **Website:** www.fultonpublishers.co.uk

English

Language Development
Circle Time Sessions to Improve Communication Skills
£17.00 • 144pp
1-84312-156-5 • 2003

OUT NOW!

Language Development
Activities for Home
£12.00 • 144pp
1-84312-170-0 • January 2004

Maths

Language Development for Maths
Circle Time Sessions to Improve Language Skills
£18.00 • 144pp
1-84312-171-9 • August 2004

Aug 2004!

Language Development for Maths
Activities for Home
£12.00 • 144pp
1-84312-172-7 • August 2004

Science

Language Development for Science
Circle Time Sessions to Improve Language Skills
£18.00 • 144pp
1-84312-173-5 • March 2005

March 2005

Language Development for Science
Activities for Home
£12.00 • 144 pp
1-84312-174-3 • March 2005

Sample activities for school

Sample activities for home

ORDER FORM

Qty	ISBN	Title	Price	Subtotal
	1-84312-156-5	Language Development	£17.00	
	1-84312-170-0	Language Development	£12.00	
	1-84312-171-9	Language Development for Maths	£18.00	
	1-84312-172-7	Language Development Maths	£12.00	
	1-84312-173-5	Language Development for Science	£18.00	
	1-84312-174-3	Language Development Science	£12.00	
			P&P	
			TOTAL	

Free p&p for Schools, LEAs and other Organisations.

Payment

☐ Please invoice
(applicable to schools, LEAs and other institutions)
Invoices will be sent from our distributor, HarperCollins Publishers

☐ I enclose a cheque payable to David Fulton Publishers Ltd
(include postage and packing)

☐ Please charge to my credit card (Visa/MasterCard, American Express, Switch, Delta)

card number ☐☐☐☐ ☐☐☐☐ ☐☐☐☐ ☐☐☐☐ ☐☐☐☐

expiry date ☐☐ ☐☐

(Switch customers only) valid from ☐☐ ☐☐   issue number ☐

IDEAS FOR HOME

Play the hiding under game

Early Years
Date:...........

Session One: Understanding the word 'under'

Get your child's duvet or sheet, put it on the floor and ask them to go UNDER it.

Say 'You are under the Duvet'. Take a turn yourself to sit under the duvet / sheet. Say I'm under too'.

Use the word 'under' and show your child things under as much as you can this week.

Please complete delivery details

Name: ....

Organisation:................................

....

Address: ....

....

....

....

Postcode: ....

Tel: ....

To order

Send to:
David Fulton Publishers, The Chiswick Centre, 414 Chiswick High Road, London W4 5TF

Freephone: 0500 618 052   **Fax:** 020 8996 3622